John D'Wolf

A voyage to the North Pacific

and a journey through Siberia, more than half a century ago

John D'Wolf

A voyage to the North Pacific
and a journey through Siberia, more than half a century ago

ISBN/EAN: 9783744745161

Printed in Europe, USA, Canada, Australia, Japan

Cover: Foto ©Andreas Hilbeck / pixelio.de

More available books at **www.hansebooks.com**

VOYAGE TO THE NORTH PACIFIC

AND

A JOURNEY THROUGH SIBERIA

MORE THAN HALF A CENTURY AGO.

BY CAPTAIN JOHN D'WOLF.

CAMBRIDGE:
WELCH, BIGELOW, AND COMPANY,
PRINTERS TO THE UNIVERSITY.
1861.

PREFACE.

My only object in combining the reminiscences and memoranda of my first voyage as shipmaster into a connected narrative, is to leave some slight record of that voyage in my family. Although I am not one of those who regard everything beyond the smoke of their own chimneys as marvellous, I think my expedition to the Northwest Coast was made a little remarkable from the circumstance that I met at Norfolk Sound his Excellency Baron von Resanoff, to whom I sold my vessel, and then crossed the North Pacific in a little craft of twenty-five tons burden, and after an overland journey of fifty-five hundred miles returned home by the way of St Petersburg. This was a voyage and travels more than half a century ago, and I was probably the first American who passed through Siberia. I know that others have claimed to be the first, and have published descriptions of the country; but I had gone over the same route before any of these claimants were born. I have often regretted that I did not make any note of what I saw, and that I had not the requisite qualifications to write an extended account of it; but business called my thoughts in other directions. I must now be content to give this imperfect sketch, the materials of which are drawn principally from memory.

VOYAGE.

I.

THE SHIP JUNO. — HER OUTFIT. — AND VOYAGE TO THE NORTHWEST COAST.

I COMMENCED a seafaring life at the early age of thirteen, and followed it through all its changes, continually rising in rank, until I reached my twenty-fourth year. Then, after a series of long voyages to the eastward of the Cape of Good Hope as chief mate, in the summer of 1804 I returned to my native town, resolved on a short respite of a few months from a close application of eleven years. I had enjoyed this leisure but a little while, however, when my employers, Messrs. Charles, James, and George D'Wolf, purchased a fine ship, called the Juno, of about two hundred and fifty tons burden, and projected a voyage to the Northwest Coast of America to collect furs for the China market. They proposed that I should take the command. I had no expectation of such an offer, since I thought myself too young and inexperienced to enter upon an entirely new branch of trade, and entertained some misgivings of my qualifications for such an enterprise. At the same time I could not so far doubt my abilities as to neglect so advantageous an opportunity, and I therefore accepted the trust.

Having engaged in the undertaking, we lost no time in making the necessary arrangements, in procuring a cargo suitable for traffic, and in preparing the vessel for the voyage. When ready for sea, the Juno and her lading were valued at $35,000. The Juno at that day was considered a crack ship, and her outfit embraced all that was needed for both comfort and convenience. She mounted eight carriage guns, and was otherwise armed in proportion, and when hauled into the stream presented quite a formidable and warlike appearance. Such an equipment was essential in her time for the dangerous business for which she was destined. The crew also would now be considered too large for a craft of the same tonnage, — for it numbered twenty-six men and boys, viz.: Samuel G. Newell, First Mate; John A. Thomas, Second Mate; James

Moorfield, Clerk; Richard Cammett, Joseph Hooper, Armorers; Thomas Hunt, Boatswain; John Jones, Carpenter; D. Bucklin, E. Bucklin, W. H. Tripp, D. Tatton, J. Stokes, J. Wheeler, W. Foy, J. Marshall, J. D. Cook, W. Phipps, J. Wheesner, J. Powers, S. Patterson, Seamen; J. Hanson, Cook; E. D. Parker, Musician; R. Hitchcock, Tailor; T. Murphy, J. Mahoney, boys. Thus manned and equipped, we took leave of our friends, weighed anchor, and put to sea on the 13th of August, 1804.

Having now fairly embarked again on the ocean, which had become a home to me, I began immediately to attend to those duties which its dangers imposed. Our anchors and cables were soon stowed away, the crew divided, the watch set, and everything prepared for all winds and weathers. We sailed in a southeasterly direction, with light breezes, and for a number of days nothing varied the monotony which the sea wears to those who have been long accustomed to it. On the 20th of September we saw at a distance St. Antonio, one of the Cape de Verde Islands. We then bent our course to the south, and were favored with fine leading winds until we reached that region of the ocean between the northeast and southeast trade-winds, which is doomed to perpetual squalls and calms, thunder, lightning, and rain. This vexatious weather was the source of one advantage, however. It afforded an opportunity for filling our water-casks, which was essential in the long voyage and moderate progress we were making.

On the 9th of November we crossed the equator in longitude 24° W. Fifty-six days to the line! Well, this certainly seems to be a long passage in comparison with those made in more modern times by the straight course pointed out by Lieut. Maury. Yet the difference is not so very extraordinary, when we consider the improvements in the sciences of navigation and naval architecture. Clippers may pursue a route with impunity which was not so safe or practicable for the square-built, seven-knot ships of half a century ago. The straight course was by no means unknown in those days, and it was sometimes followed; but with dull sailing vessels it was necessary to be more cautious, and make their "easting" while in the region of variable winds. That we crossed the Atlantic, in my time, thrice, as it is said, in going to the Cape of Good Hope, I deny. A majority of the passages made by the circuitous track would compare favorably with those made now by the same class of ships, notwithstanding the superior knowledge of winds and currents, and the numerous nautical instruments of which sea-captains avail themselves. At all events, navigation is not now carried on with more, if as much safety as formerly. Inducements are held out, in these go-ahead days, to make quick passages, regardless of ship and cargo, and the interests of the underwriters. Too implicit reliance is placed on instruments and figures at the expense of that most essential point in navigation, a vigilant lookout, and to the neglect of the use of the lead.

October 10th. We fell in with a large Spanish ship from Havana for Rio Janeiro, ninety days out. Being now several degrees in south latitude, the weather was serene and the sea smooth; there was a fine breeze from the southeast. On the 12th, we spoke a Portuguese ship from Oporto, also bound to Rio Janeiro. She had a large number of passengers on board, many of whom were sick, as they were destitute of all kinds of vegetables. I supplied them with potatoes and onions, for which they were very grateful, and presented in return a quantity of Port wine. A continuance of the pleasant weather enabled us to make various repairs in the rigging, which had been drenched and buffeted by incessant tempests to the north of the line. The change seemed to put new life and animation into the whole crew. All hands were actively employed with a good will in their various departments, — the armorers at the forge, the carpenter fitting the boats for service on the coast, the sailmakers upon the sails. Thus the vessel was put in fine condition for meeting the rough gales of Cape Horn. These we began to encounter in lat. 40° S.

November 12th, lat. 48° S., long. 51° W., we fell in with the ship Mary, of Boston, Capt. Trescott, bound to the Northwest Coast of America, and I agreed to keep company with him until we had doubled the Cape. This arrangement could be no impediment to our progress, as our vessels were nearly equal sailers. — November 15th, we saw the Falkland Islands bearing from southeast to southwest, fifteen miles distant. From our longitude we judged ourselves to be nearer the western extremity, but the wind inclining westward compelled us to pass to the eastward of them. — November 19th, the wind from the westward increased to a gale, with a heavy swell, which brought both ships under short sail. At eight, P. M., the Mary bore upon our weather quarter, about two miles distant. At ten, the wind continuing the same, I left the deck, charging the officer of the watch to be careful that we did not approach each other too near. At daylight it was perceived that she had approached us considerably, though she still held a position on the weather quarter at a sufficient distance to be out of danger. But through inattention of the officer on board the Mary to the steering, she was brought under our lee within hail; of this I was not informed by the mate in command on the deck. The Juno was making but slow progress through the water, being under short sail, with a heavy sea running, and obliged to keep close to the wind in order to avoid a collision. In this way, the ship's headway would be so checked that she would fall off two or three points, regardless of the helm. While thus situated, the Mary was in the act of coming to, and the Juno falling off, when, before either ship had gained sufficient headway to be under quick command of the helm, our whole broadsides came into contact with a crash that made every timber quake. I immediately rushed on deck, and beheld with amazement our perilous situation. In which, spite of all our efforts to get clear, we remained nearly fifteen minutes, cutting and tearing up our bulwarks, channels, and plank-sheer, and making sad work with our rigging. Finally we separated, and without apparently sustaining any injury below our plank-sheer.

This may be an uninteresting matter for record to many, but it is one of those casualties which not unfrequently occur from a reckless neglect, or a want of ordinary judgment, and yet where no one is willing to acknowledge himself at fault. They show that caution is to be regarded as a cardinal point of practical navigation. I am bold to say, that, if I had been apprised of our proximity, the collision would never have taken place.

When endeavoring to extricate the two ships, Mr. Stetson, first mate of the Mary, while on a poise upon her railing, to save himself from falling overboard, made a leap for the Juno, and landed on her deck. In the course of the day the weather became more moderate, and we put him aboard his own ship and continued our course without attempting to keep company with her. We were favored with mild weather until the 24th, which brought us into lat. 56° S. Here commenced a series of very severe gales from the westward, which continued with unabated violence for ten days. On the 5th of December the wind veered to the southward, which enabled us to make some progress, so that on the 10th I judged myself fairly to the north and west of the Cape, and a fine southwest wind was carrying us fast from it. On the 13th, as luck would have it, we fell in again with our old consort, the Mary, and sailed along with her until the 29th. Being then in lat. 44° S. and long. 85° W., I deemed it expedient to hold a consultation with my officers on the propriety of touching upon the coast of Chili, in preference to the Sandwich Islands, which was our previous intention. This was thought advisable on account of the damage sustained during our boisterous passage of one hundred and thirty-eight days. The copper on the ship's bottom, which had been worn as thin as paper during a previous long voyage of three years, had now become full of holes, and was torn off in many places by whole sheets. This and other injuries which could not be repaired at sea, in addition to the fact that all our fuel was consumed except that stowed under the cargo, and on this account we had for some time been obliged to dispense with cooking oftener than once a week, induced us to part company again with the Mary, and shape our course for Concepcion. I was well aware of the natural and deep-rooted jealousy of the Spaniards; but while I apprehended trouble on this score, I was determined to find admittance to some port, after having relinquished my original scheme of visiting the Sandwich Islands.

On the 1st of January, 1805, at 2 P. M., we saw land bearing from southeast to northeast, fifteen miles distant, and shortly after the island of St. Maria. At the same time we saw a ship standing out from the shore, which we spoke. She was a whaler from New Bedford. The wind was blowing so hard that we could learn nothing further. At sunset it had died away, and left us still four or five miles off Concepcion. As it was not practicable to make the harbor in the night-time, we tacked ship and stood out from the coast, with a view to holding our situation to the windward until morning, and at midnight we tacked and stood in again. At daybreak, however, we found the current had set us a considerable distance north of our port. I accordingly resolved to make sail for Valparaiso; since that was the principal port in Chili, we had reason to anticipate a better reception than at any place of less note, where our presence might have excited unjust suspicions of unlawful trade. Our sole object was to repair our vessel and obtain supplies for our voyage, and these by the laws of humanity they could not in justice refuse us.

The weather continued remarkably serene and pleasant, with light breezes and frequent calms; and as we coasted along within eight or ten miles of the shore, we had a most splendid view of the Andes, towering far above the clouds. On the morning of the 8th, we entered the bay of Valparaiso. Before we reached a safe anchorage, we were visited by an officer from the Governor, who requested to know who we were, whence we came, and the object of our visit, — all of which I explained to his apparent satisfaction. The boat then returned to the shore with a message to the Governor, while the officer remained on board, saying that he could not suffer us to anchor until he received orders. But before the boat returned, the ship had reached the anchorage ground, and we came to immediately, notwithstanding his remonstrances. The boat brought a peremptory command to leave the bay; but this was out of the question, and so I as peremptorily refused. I was summoned before the Governor to present my papers for examination, and account for my conduct. After examining my invoices and other documents, and listening to a candid explanation of the reasons which induced me to come into port, he was convinced that my destination was the Northwest Coast. I was accordingly permitted to remain until I received further orders from the Governor-General, at St. Jago, to whom a messenger was despatched. In the mean time I was allowed to take on board as much wood and water, and fresh provisions, as I chose. The harbor was too rough and exposed to make the repairs we needed, and therefore we weighed anchor and sailed for Coquimbo, where we arrived on the 20th, and dropped anchor in six fathoms of water, on the west side of the bay, about eight miles from the town. Here we remained until the 28th, when, having completed our repairs as far as practicable, we put to sea with a fine breeze from the south.

When we reached 4° S. lat., we had series of calms, with pleasant weather, and a very smooth sea. In this neighborhood we saw great numbers of green turtle, and by capturing several we added a delicacy to our larder. February 20th, between 9 and 11 A. M., I obtained several distances of the sun and moon, the mean of which made the long. 108° W.; at meridian, I found we had crossed the equator into north latitude.

The wind continued very light and variable until the 4th of March, when it inclined to the northeast. On the 16th, we crossed the Tropic of Cancer. At this point the winds again became variable and squally. On the 7th of April, we had strong gales and threatening sky, with rain at intervals. At 8 P. M. of that date I put the ship under short sail, and hauled upon the wind to the northward, deeming it imprudent to continue on our course through the night, because, by my calculations, we were in the vicinity of land. In the morning the weather moderated, and at 5 A. M. we saw land bearing from north-northeast to east, which proved to be the northern part of Vancouver's Island. At 2 P. M. we saw Scott's Island bearing north-northwest, sixteen miles distant. At nightfall the clouds wore an ugly look; so we hauled by the wind to the westward, under short sail. At midnight we had a heavy blow, but it died away by light, and we saw Scott's Island again; at 9 A. M. it bore south, five miles. The wind beginning again to rise, I determined if possible to make a harbor before night. With this intention I shaped my course for Newettee.

Newettee was a small inlet in the northwestern promontory of Vancouver's Island, and sheltered from the sea by a long island running nearly east and west. Between the two was a strait, through which we must enter to gain our port. As we drew near the entrance, the wind became very light, and at sunset we were still three miles from it. Being myself entirely unacquainted with the coast, I was inclined to lay off until morning; but my officers were all more or less familiar with it, and so positive of their knowledge that I concluded to proceed. At eight in the evening we crossed the bar at the mouth of the strait, and entered. The wind had fallen now to a dead calm, and left us exposed to a very strong current, which carried us toward an inlet in the island to the north of us; and at the same time it was evident that we were approaching the shore very fast. Nothing could surpass the terrific appearance of the scenery; perpendicular cliffs towered from the water's edge to a lofty height, against which the sea beat with great violence. The ship getting no steerage-way from her sails, and being in fact entirely unmanageable, we hoisted out our boats to tow. The long-boat, which was of the most consequence, sunk alongside; the yawl and the whale-boat were both got ahead, but were so light that they had very little effect on the vessel. We were now within three rods of a high projecting point, and the soundings showed forty-five fathoms of water. We let go the kedge-anchor to keep the bow off, and it had the desired effect. By great exertions in the boats, assisted in the ship by the application of all the oars we had, we barely succeeded in keeping clear of the rocks, which could now be reached with an oar. As the tide swept us along, we were threatened with destruction by every sea which dashed against them. At length, by the aid of a light air which sprung up, we got out of the irregular current near the shore, and, slipping our cable and leaving our anchor, moved towards the harbor on the south side of the straits. When about two thirds of the way across, I despatched a boat with an officer to find the entrance. The boat not returning in due time, I discharged a musket as a signal. It was answered from a vessel lying within, and shortly after one of the officers came aboard from her, and informed us that it was the ship Pearl of Boston, Capt. Ebbets. He very politely offered to pilot us in, and by his assistance we were soon brought safely to anchor in fifteen fathoms of water. This was the 10th of April, 1805.

II.

Newettee and the Natives. — Kygarney. — Norfolk Sound. — Sell Part of my Cargo to the Russians. — Governor Baranoff. — Chatham Straits. — Newettee again. — Return to Chatham Straits. — Trade with the Indians. — On the Rocks. — Sail to Norfolk Sound for Repairs. — Arrival of Resanoff and Party. — The Juno sold to the Russians. — Departure of my Crew for Canton.

At last I was at anchor on the Northwest Coast. Newettee was one of the southernmost harbors frequented by American fur-traders, being in lat. 51° N., and long. 128° W. It was nothing more than a nook, as I said before, in the northern end of Vancouver's Island. We found it tolerably well sheltered from all winds except those from the north and northeast; on this quarter it was exposed to a reach of about three miles. As the prevalent wind during our stay of ten days was from the south and southwest, we lay in perfect safety, notwithstanding it was one continued gale, accompanied with hail and rain. Everything around us, the sea, the sky, and the precipitous shore, covered with a forest of heavy timber, wore a most gloomy aspect. The Indians had no permanent residence here, but made it merely a place of resort for traffic on the arrival of ships. For this purpose it was considered at certain seasons one of the best harbors on the coast, as there are many large villages in its vicinity. We were visited daily by a great number of the Indians, who generally brought with them a few sea-otter skins, but not enough to make trade brisk. They were exceedingly sharp in all their intercourse with us, being great beggars, withal. It seemed impossible to satisfy them for their skins, and they were ready to grasp at everything they saw. They were a very stout and robust people, and in some things not destitute of skill. Their boats were hewn from a single log, and varied in size from sixteen feet in length and three in breadth, to thirty-five in length and six in breadth. Their paddles were made and ornamented with a great deal of neatness.

Deriving but little benefit from our traffic, we employed ourselves in putting the ship in good order for beating about the coast. By the 20th we had completed our work, and weighed anchor, and put to sea in company with the Pearl, directing our course to the northward for Kygarney, a harbor in lat. 54° 30′ N., which, from its central situation, is considered the best place of resort for ships on their first arrival, to obtain information for establishing a rate of trade. For several days we sailed in a thick fog, which, lifting at intervals, showed us different points of Queen Charlotte's Island. We gained our port on the 27th, and found there the ships Vancouver, Captain Brown, and Caroline, Captain Sturgis, both of Boston; the latter, having obtained her cargo, about to leave the coast for Canton.

During our stay here we got in a new mizenmast in place of the old one, which was sprung, and furnished our vessel with such other spars as we thought we should need. We were daily visited by the Indians, who generally brought a few skins; but they were so extravagant in their demands for them that it was impossible to trade. We frequently had thirty or forty lying about the decks the whole day long, endeavoring to extort unreasonable prices for their furs, at the same time affecting the utmost indifference whether they sold them or not. Occasionally they were quite insulting; but policy induced us to put up with insults, in hopes of driving a bargain.

The numerous inlets in the vicinity abounded with salmon, and every other variety of fish, and wild game was very plenty. But on the whole the harbor was poor and unsafe. The land here, as at Newettee, was exceedingly elevated, rising abruptly from the shore, and covered with heavy timber, chiefly of the fir kind. The water is very deep, which compelled a vessel to anchor so near the land as to be exposed to any hostile demonstration on the part of the savages. Attacks were not rare when only one ship was in port. From long intercourse with American traders, the natives had become extremely expert in the use of the musket, in the choice of which they showed great judgment and sagacity, and invariably selected a king's arm in preference to the most finished fowling-piece. On account of the many instances of bloodshed by them, they were not allowed to come on board armed, but it was necessary to show them every indulgence within the bounds of prudence.

Not being likely to receive much benefit from a longer stay here, I resolved to proceed at once to the settlement of the Russians on Norfolk Sound, since a great part of my cargo consisted of articles adapted to their use. We had rum, tobacco, molasses, sugar, rice, wooden ware, duffels, &c., which the Indians will take only as presents, as well as those commodities intended for trade with them, viz. blankets, muskets, powder, and balls.

On the 7th of May we put to sea, with pleasant weather and a moderate breeze from the west, and directed our course to the northward. On the 8th, the wind increased to a gale, and veered to the south, which brought thick fog and rain. On the 9th it became clear, and we obtained a good view of the land, and discovered that we were near the entrance of the sound, about mid-channel, with Mount Edgecombe bearing northwest, ten miles distant. We stood in under a press of sail, and at about eleven came to anchor in Magee's Harbor, as it was called, on the west side of the sound. We found erected on the shore a guide-post, pointing out the direction of the village, and the date of its establishment. We were soon visited by several baidarkas* with Kodiak Indians, from whom we endeavored to obtain information. The only word they used, which we could understand, was

---

* Leather canoes. They consist of a skeleton of wood, over which is stretched a covering made of the skins of sea-lions. They are long and narrow, and hold from one to three persons. Each person sits in a round hole just fitted to the size of the body.

Baranoff, which we knew to be the name of the governor or superintendent of the settlement. As soon as the news of our arrival in the sound reached there, a pilot was despatched to our assistance, and, the wind being favorable, he brought us round to the village, and we anchored on the 10th of May abreast of the fort.

Mr. Abraham Jones, an American in the Russian service, immediately came on board, with the Governor's compliments, and kind offers of protection, and any aid we might need which it was in his power to give. Accompanied by Mr. Moorfield, I accepted an invitation to go on shore and have an interview with him. Mr. Jones officiated as interpreter. I was introduced by him to his Excellency, and received with every mark of friendship and hospitality. After exchanging the usual compliments, we were ushered into an apartment where we found a table spread with all the luxuries the place afforded. While we regaled ourselves with the sumptuous fare, the conversation turned to the subject of my cargo. The Governor appeared willing and desirous to exchange furs on fair terms for such articles as they needed. We returned on board in the evening, well pleased with our reception, I might say agreeably disappointed, as I had been led to believe from various reports that we should find the Russians little advanced from the savage state.

As the success of my voyage depended on the utmost possible despatch, no time was lost in establishing a rate of exchange with our new friends; which being adjusted to our mutual advantage, I was enabled to disencumber the vessel of a large portion of the bulkiest part of my cargo,— such as has been mentioned on a preceding page.

From the kind treatment received from the Governor, I was induced to form a very favorable opinion of him. He was sixty-five years of age, and had spent the last eighteen years of his life at different stations on the coast, in the capacity of agent and officer of the Russian American Company,— excluded, as it were, from all civilized society, except that of a few of his fellow-adventurers. He possessed a strong mind, easy manners and deportment, and was apparently well fitted for the place he filled. He commanded the greatest respect from the Indians, who regarded him with mingled feelings of love and fear.

Owing to frequent storms of rain, which unavoidably retarded the progress of our business, my stay at this place was prolonged until the 27th of May. With pleasant weather and a moderate breeze we then weighed anchor, and sailed from Norfolk Sound. We proceeded up Chatham Straits as high as Lynn Canal, in lat. 59° N., thence southward to Newettee in lat. 51° N., touching at as many of the intermediate harbors as we found it practicable, and making some trade. We arrived at Newettee on the 28th of June, at the same time with the brig Lydia and the ships Vancouver and Athawalpa. The latter had been attacked by the Indians, who killed Capt. Porter and all the officers, and wounded many of the sailors. She had fallen in with the other ship and brig, belonging to the same owners, and had proceeded to this place for assistance. Here we found the Pearl and the Mary.

I shall not attempt a detail of the occurrences, or give a description of the harbors and inlets we visited in our voyage from Norfolk Sound. While here we rendered all the assistance in our power in manning and equipping the Athawalpa for Canton, and then, on the 11th of July, again left Newettee and sailed northward for Chatham Straits. Touching at a number of places on our passage, on the 27th we entered the mouth of the straits, and proceeded up as far as Point Retreat in lat. 58° N. Here the Indians were very numerous, and appeared to have a great number of skins for sale, but declined trading, unless we brought the ship to anchor, which was unnecessary, as the wind was light and the sea smooth. There was nothing to interrupt a traffic if they really felt willing to open one; but, in order to comply with their wishes as far as possible, I made several attempts to get an anchorage, and was only prevented by the depth of the water. Still the Indians kept round us in great numbers, there being at least thirty or forty canoes of them. At the same time we perceived that they were all armed, and this, with their obstinacy, gave us strong suspicions that they were bent on mischief more than commerce. As it was nearly sunset, and there was no prospect of bringing them to terms, I concluded to make the best of my way down the straits. The wind was light, and the tide against us. The Indians, seeing plainly that we could make but little progress in the course of the night, went on shore, and returned at daylight. They came with the apparent determination to board us; but in their absence we had made ample preparations to meet in a hostile as well as a friendly manner. Seeing the impossibility of obtaining access to the ship by force, they changed their tactics, and were inclined to trade with us in a peaceable way. We therefore admitted one of the chiefs at the gangway, and through him commenced a brisk traffic, which continued until we had bought their whole stock of furs. They then left us to continue our course down the straits without molestation.

On the 5th of August we came to anchor in an extensive harbor, situated near the entrance of Chatham Straits, between Points Sullivan and Ellis. Here we were detained several days by calms and light westerly winds, which blew directly into the harbor, while the entrance was so narrow that we found it impossible to beat out. On the 10th we got under weigh, with the boats ahead to tow; but the ebb tide began to run very strong, and drift the ship towards a small island lying midway in the channel. Notwithstanding our utmost efforts to avoid it by the use of oars and letting go an anchor, in the darkness which had come on we had approached nearer the shore than we supposed, and finally the keel struck upon the rocks. The stream anchor was carried out with all possible despatch in order to heave the vessel off, but in vain. The falling tide had left her too fast. The only alternative left was to secure her in the best manner possible before she began to keel over, and to prepare ourselves for defence in case of an attack from the savages. Having furled all the sails, sent down the topgallant yards and masts, and lashed our heavy guns amidship, we equipped our three boats with arms, ammunition, and provision, lest the ship should bilge, which we had great reason to apprehend, as we had still on board about two thirds of our cargo. But as the tide left her we found that she did not lie so much on her beam-ends as we had anticipated, but was supported by three sharp rocks, one about midships, and the other two abreast the fore and mizzen chains; her keel had also taken the rocks in several places.

At sunrise the Indians began to assemble about us. At first they kept aloof, and seemed to entertain some suspicions as to our movements; but after going round the ship and examining her situation very carefully, we prevailed upon some of them to come alongside. We gave them to understand that we had hauled on shore to mend the copper; and to convince them, I employed a gang of hands under the ship's bottom for that purpose. At 9 A. M. we had low water, and as the perpendicular rise and fall of the tide was about fifteen feet, we could now walk all round the vessel, and under the keel in some places. In the mean time some of the officers were employed in trading with the Indians for their furs; and to make ourselves secure in case they had any hostile intentions, we succeeded in enticing one of the chiefs on board, whom we detained as a hostage. Thus relieved in a measure from any apprehension of an attack from the natives, and having done everything in our power to ease the ship, we lost no time in caulking and stopping in the best possible manner such places as had been strained open by her ponderous weight upon the rocks. The two seams below the plank-sheer were nearly an inch wide, as likewise every butt from the fore to the mizzenmast. To clear the bilge of the ship we rigged one of our pumps in the main hatchway, and drew out a considerable quantity of molasses and water. After some brisk work, we had the satisfaction of finding that the vessel righted with the flowing tide, and at high water, to our great joy, she floated. When we hauled into the stream again, we were happy to find that she did not leak so badly as we had reason to anticipate. The only perceptible injury was on the side which laid on the rocks, and that was bent or hogged up, as the phrase is, about half a foot. We now liberated our hostage, after making him a very liberal present for his detention.

While we were aground, we had a favorable opportunity to examine the copper on the ship's bottom, which proved to be in a very shattered condition; and as we had reason to apprehend more damage than was visible, I deemed it advisable to proceed at once to the Russian settlement at Norfolk Sound, where, under protection from the Indians, we might discharge our cargo, and make repairs in peace. Accordingly, on the 12th of August we put to sea, and made the best of our way for that place. On our route we fell in again with the Mary, and, in company with her, arrived on the 14th, and anchored abreast the village. I was again received by Governor Baranoff with that kind and obliging hospitality which made him loved and respected by every visitor.

No time was lost in preparing to lay the Juno on shore, in order to ascertain the extent of the damage. In this I was greatly facilitated by the Governor, who allowed me to occupy an old hulk, into which I shifted my cargo, with the exception of the furs. We had collected about a thousand sea-otter skins, and these I sent to Canton by the Mary, which sailed on the 20th. Notwithstanding our utmost exertions, our preparations were not completed until the 1st of September, and then, to my great surprise and regret, I found twenty of the floor timbers broken, and the copper in a very ragged condition. I was, however, gratified to find the planks all sound and good except in one place, where the carpenter cut out a large fragment of the rock, which had penetrated the bottom, and adhered so closely as to prevent the admission of water. By the 6th of September we had completed such repairs as were practicable and hauled into the stream, knowing no other alternative than to make the best of our crippled ship, and endeavor to prosecute the remainder of our voyage with more caution.

Having again adjusted the rigging, replenished our stores of wood and water, and put everything in the best possible trim for sea, I submitted to Governor Baranoff a project of an expedition to the southern coast of New Albion and California, which he readily accepted. My idea was to take on board fifty or sixty Kodiak Indians, with their canoes, for the purpose of catching sea-otter, those animals being very numerous on that coast.

Everything in this new plan being agreed upon and settled, we were to wait until the 1st of October for the Indians, who were out on a hunting expedition, under the protection of two small vessels, and expected to return by the last of the month.

While we were waiting, the Russian brig Maria arrived at the settlement. She was under the command of Andrew W. Maschin, a lieutenant in the navy, and had on board as passenger Nicholas Resanoff, a nobleman, who, after an unsuccessful embassy to Japan, returned to Kamtchatka *en route* to the posts on the Northwest Coast belonging to the Russian American Company, in which he was himself a large proprietor. With him came also two other lieutenants in the Russian navy, Nicholas Schwostoff and John Davidoff, Doctor Geo. Langsdorff, and two ship-carpenters, Messrs. Korükin and Popoff, who were to build a ship at this place. To all these new-comers I was formally introduced by my friend the Governor, and received the assurances of his Excellency, Baron von Resanoff, that he would facilitate, in every way in his power, the execution of my California scheme. Several days after this arrival were passed in festivity and mirth, and business was entirely suspended. The appearance of so distinguished a personage, whose authority was for a time to supersede even that of the Governor, was an event of great moment.

In conversation with Dr. Langsdorff on the inconvenience of building and equipping a large vessel where the necessary materials were so difficult to procure, I observed to him, jocosely, that I would sell them my ship, which would obviate the necessity of building. The conversation being communicated to his Excellency, he wished to know whether I would really sell my ship, and if so, what would be the price. This was a subject on which I had not reflected, and which required some deliberation on several accounts. Having about two thirds of my cargo on board, it was necessary to ascertain of what it consisted to estimate its value, being well aware that I could not dispose of my vessel by itself alone. How my officers and crew were to leave the coast was another serious difficulty. But while I was deliberating on the expediency of the measure, the two small vessels, the Yermerk and Russisloff, which I mentioned above, returned from the hunting expedition. The former, a craft of forty tons, appeared to be suitable for my purpose, and I therefore availed myself of the opportunity, and offered my ship, and the remainder of my cargo, for the sum of $68,000, payable in the following manner, viz.: bills of exchange on the Directors of the Russian American Company at St. Petersburg for the sum of $54,638; 572 sea-otter skins for the sum of $13,062; and $300 in cash; together with the fore-named vessel, the Yermerk, completely rigged, two suits of sails, four carriage guns, thirty muskets, with ammunition for the same, and provisions for my crew for one hundred days. This offer was accepted, and the Juno passed into the hands of the Russian American Company. On the 5th of October, I delivered her up, under a salute from the fort and the ship, when I hoisted the stars and stripes on the Yermerk, which had become my property.

Having consummated our bargain by delivering up our ship, and taking possession of our little craft, we set to work immediately to put her into a condition to transport ourselves and the sea-otter skins to Canton. This work was completed by the 15th; and while we were waiting for favorable weather to put to sea, his Excellency suggested to me the advisability of despatching the Yermerk for Canton, and remaining myself at the settlement until spring, and then embarking with himself and suite for Ochotsk, and proceeding to St. Petersburg by land. The kind and courteous manner in which this proposition was made to me was too flattering to be received with indifference. After duly considering the subject, having in view the probable advantage of presenting my bills of exchange in person the next winter, in accordance with the advice of my friends, I concluded to avail myself of his Excellency's generous offer. I therefore gave the command of the Yermerk to my first officer, Mr. George W. Stetson, and the superintendence of the business to Mr. James Moorfield. Storms and adverse winds prevented them from sailing until the 27th, when, with a favorable breeze, they took their departure from Norfolk Sound, with our most fervent prayers for their welfare and safe arrival at Canton.

After taking a long parting look at the little vessel fading in the horizon, I returned to the village, full of melancholy forebodings of a tedious and dreary winter in that rude and inhospitable region. But it was of no use to repine; the business was settled, and I concluded I would take things as they came, and make the best of them. I had retained in my service, as valet, Edward D. Parker, one of my ordinary sailors, but a very useful man of all work. A barber by trade, he was also a tolerably good tailor, and performer on the violin and clarinet. This latter accomplishment I thought might be useful in dispelling the blues, if we should at any time be troubled with that complaint. An apartment was assigned me by the Governor, adjoining the room of Dr. Langsdorff, to which I removed my goods and chattels. I had a sleeping bunk fitted up in one corner, and made everything as comfortable as possible for a long siege. Having thus taken up my residence among the Russians, I will pause to make some explanations connected with my narrative.

III.

NICHOLAS RESANOFF AND THE JAPAN EXPEDITION. — THE HISTORY OF THE RUSSIAN SETTLEMENT AT NORFOLK SOUND AND THE FOUNDING OF NEW ARCHANGEL. — THE CHINESE PROJECT. — DR. LANGSDORFF AND OTHER NEW FRIENDS. — VISIT TO THE INDIANS DRIVEN BY THE RUSSIANS FROM ARCHANGEL.

IN September, 1803, an expedition sailed from Cronstadt, Russia, for the Pacific Ocean, consisting of the two ships Nadeschda and Neva, the former commanded by Capt. Krusenstern, and the latter by Capt. Lisiansky, both experienced officers of the Imperial navy. This was the first adventure the Russians ever attempted in the Southern Ocean, and was prompted by the extension of the trade of the Russian American Fur Company. It had the double purpose of supplying the settlements on the Northwest Coast, and negotiating a commercial treaty with Japan, which, being near the settlements, would be a convenient place to obtain provisions and dispose of commodities. Encouragement had been given by a letter received many years previous from the Japanese, granting permission to come to the port of Nangasaki; on the strength of this letter, and in view of the advantages and facilities for intercourse, it was thought expedient by the Imperial government to send an embassy to this strange people. Accordingly, Nicholas Resanoff, a nobleman and Chamberlain to his Majesty, the Emperor of all the Russias, was appointed, and embarked in the Nadeschda, with powers plenipotentiary to negotiate with the Court of Jedo. This part of the undertaking, as is well known, proved a failure. After remaining at Nangasaki six months, subject a part of the time to a partial imprisonment, and throughout to absurd formalities and ridiculous vexations, he despaired of bringing about a favorable result, and was compelled to depart for Kamtchatka, without even obtaining an interview with the Emperor, and, in fact, accomplishing nothing.

Baron von Resanoff was a person of rank and distinction, possessed of many amiable qualities, and highly esteemed by the Emperor Alexander. He was kind and affable to all around him, and always ready to hear complaints, and afford every redress in his power for grievances. He married the daughter of the famous Schelikoff, who was the pioneer in the Russian discoveries and settlements on the Northwest Coast. This circumstance caused him to be largely interested in the Fur Company. His mission to Japan having terminated unfavorably, his intention then was to visit and inspect all the stations of the Company on the coast. He left the Nadeschda therefore at Kamtchatka, and embarked on board the brig Maria. After touching at various Russian establishments, he finally arrived at Norfolk Sound. The Neva, Captain Lisiansky, pursued its course directly to the island of Kodiak, and thence to Norfolk Sound, where it arrived August 20, 1804, and joined, by previous agreement, a small squadron of three vessels under the command of Governor Baranoff.

The Russians had formerly a settlement on the Sound, situated several miles from their present location, called Archangel, which was destroyed by the Indians, and all the inhabitants massacred. The Indians then established themselves on the spot, and erected strong fortifications. The object of assembling the vessels was to chastise and expel them, and this was accomplished after a siege of four days. The Russians then selected an elevated and commanding situation in the immediate vicinity. It was a singular round piece of land with a flat top, standing out in the sea, and bearing the appearance of a work of human hands. The only connection with the shore was by a narrow isthmus. Here they put up several buildings, mounted a considerable battery of heavy guns, and gave the place the name of New Archangel.

The Neva then returned to Kodiak, where she wintered, and in the fall of 1805 proceeded to Canton and rejoined the Nadeschda, which had previously sailed thither. The aim in this movement was to accomplish a third project of the Russian American Company, which, like the Japan scheme, was unsuccessful. They desired to obtain permission from the Chinese government to continue their intercourse with the port of Canton, and so enable their ships to return by sea from the settlements to Russia, with the proceeds of their furs. But the Chinese objected, and insisted on their confining themselves to their inland traffic at the north. Thus commerce for the future with Canton was interdicted. I relate these events because they took place but a short time previous to my sojourn at Norfolk Sound, and account for the presence there of several persons of distinction.

George von Langsdorff, a native of Frankfort, Germany, was by profession a doctor of medicine and surgery, and by taste a naturalist. He was a volunteer on the Russian American expedition, and was in pursuit of science. On his arrival in Kamtchatka a second time, he was invited by Baron von Resanoff to accompany him to the Northwest Coast of America, as his physician. He was particularly moved to accept the invitation by the opportunity which was thus offered for the collection of specimens of natural history. The Doctor, unlike Baron von Resanoff, spoke the English language fluently. As I lived under the same roof with him, we became almost inseparable, participating both in each others' pleasures and troubles. Lieutenants Schwostoff, Davidoff, and Maschin were highly accomplished and meritorious officers, as were likewise the two ship-builders, Messrs. Popoff and Korükin. They all seemed to vie in attention and kindness to me as their guest, and by general invitation I dined with these gentlemen at the Governor's table.

The stock of provisions at the settlement had been very small and of the poorest kind, and the increase of the population by the arrival of the Ambassador and his suite made the subject of supplies for the coming winter a matter for sober consideration; but by the purchase of the Juno they were relieved from all serious anxiety on that score, as a great part of her cargo consisted of good wholesome provisions, such as beef, pork, flour, bread, rice, sugar, molasses, rum, and tobacco. In fact, the desire to obtain these stores had great weight in their negotiations with me. There was still, however, some deficiency in inferior kinds of food, and a small vessel had been despatched some time previously to Kodiak. It was so late in the season she did not return. Now they were not afraid of winter storms, for they had the Juno to send on the errand. She sailed, under the command of Lieutenants Schwostoff and Davidoff, on the 27th of October.

In the mean while the whole village, comprising a population of 150 Russians, and perhaps 250 Aleutians, was actively engaged in preparing to meet the rigors of the approaching season. They built log-houses, work-shops, and barracks. My friend Langsdorff was all the time ranging the woods and the shores with his fowling-piece, in quest of wild game for specimens, with which, after they had been skinned for science' sake, my man Parker made stews of various descriptions. Being merely a sojourner at the settlement, I occupied myself in watching the labors of others, getting acquainted with the different characters and localities of the place, and learning the use and management of baidarkas.

By the beginning of November the novelty of our situation had worn off; the circumscribed range of our wanderings from the village became monotonous and tiresome, and, as a number of our associates had departed for Kodiak, we began to look round for some new object of interest. The Doctor had frequently expressed a desire to become more acquainted with the Sitcha Indians, and resolved on making them a visit at their village, on the opposite side of the island, if I would accompany him, to which I readily agreed. As these were the very Indians who had recently been so roughly handled by the Russians, it was considered by the Governor and other friends to be a rather perilous adventure; but we relied a good deal on our not being Russians, and upon the fact that I had been among them during the previous summer as a trader from a people with whom they were on friendly terms. Perceiving that we were bent on going, the Governor gave his consent, and furnished us with baidarkas, Kodiak Indians, and an Indian woman as an interpreter. The latter was a daughter of one of the principal chiefs of the tribe we were to visit. She had lived with the Russians five or six years, and with her as a companion we had little fear of any other than a friendly reception.

We soon completed the preparations for our departure. We took guns, pistols, powder, and shot, for shooting as well as for safety; rice, tea, sugar, biscuit, dried fish, and brandy, for our food. Beside some kitchen utensils for dressing these provisions and a small tent to sleep in, we were provided with several ells of linen and woollen cloth, glass beads, needles, tobacco, large fishing-hooks, looking-glasses, and various similar trifles for presents to the Indians. Langsdorff, the interpreter, and myself each occupied a baidarka, and had two natives each to row.

We were three days in reaching the village, but beyond a few Indians, with whom we encamped at night, we saw nothing of interest. By nightfall of the third day we had nearly reached the place of our destination; but owing to a strong wind and tide, which were directly against us, we had the mortification of seeing the sun go down before the whole distance was accomplished. We were now in rather an unpleasant situation; to return was impossible, and to land might have excited suspicion, for the fire which was necessary as a protection from the cold must have betrayed us. We determined at last to make our way to the settlement, notwithstanding we should reach it in utter darkness. Scarcely was this resolution taken, when we were observed from the land, and hailed in a loud voice, but neither our interpreter nor our Kodiak oarsmen would reply. This sorely provoked Langsdorff and myself, and we were on the point of expressing our anger warmly, when a great commotion arose on shore. Suddenly, some hundred naked Indians, armed with muskets, and holding firebrands in their hands, thronged to the water's edge. No sooner had we made known who we were, and approached the shore, than we were surrounded in a tumultuous manner by the Kaluschians, who dragged us towards their fortress, seizing upon our effects at the same time, whether to rob us of them or to restore them we were then ignorant. I expected nothing but an immediate and violent death. The scene certainly was one to inspire terror; the glare of the torches, the gesticulations of the savages, the brandishing of the weapons, the rough handling we received, were not calculated to inspire confidence in men whom from the outset we had distrusted. But happily our fears were groundless, and the demonstrations of the natives, as we afterwards learned, were well intended offices of friendship.

We were hurried over a rather fatiguing road to the top of a high rock, on which stood the fortress, and were immediately introduced into the very spacious habitation of the chief Dlchaetin, the father of our interpreter. He assigned us a place directly opposite the entrance, where we spread a carpet, and, by the light of a very large fire on a raised hearth in the centre of the room, were subjected to the gaze of some hundreds of the natives. Shortly after, to our great astonishment, our packages were brought to us from our baidarkas, not the smallest trifle being withheld, although there were undoubtedly many articles among them which the bearers must have coveted, and under the cover of the night might have easily concealed. Even my musket, pistols, and powder-horn, which in my hurry I had left behind, were delivered to me without the slightest injury.

We had scarcely refreshed ourselves with a dish of tea and a glass of punch, when we were invited by the eldest and most distinguished of the chiefs, the commandant of the fortress, to come and visit him. He received us with much kindness, and presented me with a sea-otter's skin, and Dr. Langsdorff with a beautiful sea-otter's tail. Much fatigued, and in need of rest, we returned to the habitation of our host; but we found ourselves in too exciting a scene to permit of sleep. While eating a very good dish of fish and rice prepared by him, we were entertained with a lively and pleasing melody, sung by a number of men seated round the fire, which had been piled up to a great height. Though the night was cold and windy, the savages went barefoot to the neighboring forest, and brought home large blocks of wood upon their naked shoulders, and heaped them on the hearth. It was incomprehensible how the roof, covered as it was merely with bark, was not entirely consumed. Once it did take fire; but a boy ran like a mouse up the side of the wall, and extinguished it. The sparks flew out of the opening at the top, and the flames roared as in a blacksmith's forge; and we could not close our eyes till their fierceness had in a measure subsided, and the danger was less imminent, though the fire was very hot through the whole night.

On the morning of the next day we carried to the commandant from whom we had received the presents the evening before the counter presents due to him. At the same time, we made the proper tribute of presents to the parents of our interpreter, the latter having given us to understand that the sooner it was done, the greater would be their esteem for us. To her father we gave some ells of woollen cloth, a large knife, some fish-hooks, and some pounds of tobacco; to her mother a shift, some needles, a small looking-glass, some ribbon, and some glass beads. As soon as we had performed these necessary ceremonies, we were permitted to walk about wherever we chose, without the trouble of guides. Dr. Langsdorff even shot some birds close to the fortress without attracting any attention.

The natives of the Northwest Coast of America are called by the Russians Kaluschians, but this people call themselves Schitchachon, or inhabitants of Sitcha. Expelled from Norfolk Sound, they had fortified themselves here, upon a rock which rose perpendicularly to the height of several hundred feet above the water's edge. The only possible access to it was on the northwest side, and here it had been rendered extremely difficult by very large trunks of trees strewn over it. The rock itself was secured against the attack of an enemy by a double palisade, measuring from twelve to fifteen feet in height, and from three to four in thickness. A natural wall of earth beyond the palisading, on the side towards the sea, conceals the habitations so effectually, that they cannot be discerned from a ship.

The houses within the fortress were placed in regular rows, and built of thick plank, fastened to posts which formed the frame-work, and covered at the top with bark. The entrance was at the gable end, and was often stained with different colored earths. The interiors of their dwellings were indescribably filthy, filled with smoke, and perfumed with decayed fish and train-oil. The men painted their faces, and, as well as the women, delighted in profuse ornaments; like other savages, they were particularly pleased with glittering trinkets, or European garments. The women on the coast had one very strange fashion, which I think is peculiar to this part of the world. At the age of fourteen or fifteen, they make a hole in their under lip and insert a small piece of wood like a button. This is increased in size as they advance in age, until it is three or four inches long, and one or two wide. I saw one old woman, the wife of a chief, whose lip ornament was so large, that, by a peculiar motion of her under lip, she could almost conceal her whole face with it. You will naturally inquire the reason of this barbarous method of adornment. I might reply by asking the reason of some equally strange fashions among civilized nations. But, without casting any reflections on my countrywomen, I may be allowed to make one observation, which has probably occurred already to my readers; and that is, that it is utterly impossible for the fair sex of the Northwest Coast to enjoy the luxury of a kiss.

The occupations of the Sitcha Indians, beside hunting and fishing, appeared to be making canoes, fishing-lines and hooks, and wooden ware. The women manufacture a kind of carpet out of the wool of wild sheep, and are very expert in wicker-work; some of their baskets are so closely woven as to hold water. Both sexes are expert in the use of fire-arms, and are excellent judges of their quality. I could not find that they had any organized government. Success in fishing and in the chase constitutes the source of their wealth, and consequently of their influence. In feuds between different families the right of the strongest prevails, and they are only banded together against common enemies.

Having passed two days at the Indian settlement, we set out on our return to New Archangel. On our route we visited the chief Schinchetaez, with whom we had passed a night on our way to Sitcha. This man had been friendly to the Russians, and was in consequence an outcast from his own people. He was glad to see us again, and entertained us hospitably. We gave him a few presents, which were thankfully received, and, had he been able, he would have given in return. While with him we saw some Kaluschian Indians go into the sea to bathe, when the thermometer was below freezing. They ran for some distance over the ice, and then plunged in, and performed all manner of antics, with the same apparent enjoyment as if it had been a warm spring.

After taking leave of our host we entered our baidarkas and resumed our journey; and in due time reached New Archangel and our friends, without any accident or occurrence of sufficient interest to record.

IV.

PREPARATIONS FOR WINTER. — WINTER AMUSEMENTS. — RESANOFF MAKES AN EXPEDITION TO CALIFORNIA. — BATTLE BETWEEN A WOLF AND A RAM. — I SAIL FOR OCHOTSK IN THE RUSSISLOFF.

SHORTLY after our return from the excursion narrated in the last chapter, our friends Schwostoff and Davidoff arrived from Kodiak with the Juno, and brought a considerable quantity of dried fish, oil, beans, &c., to increase our stock of winter provisions. The dried fish was called *ukler*, and was prepared by splitting and taking out the backbone of the fish, and then laying it in the sun. Thus cured, it was eaten as a substitute for bread. The people having now a fair allowance of provisions, the operations at the settlement went on quite encouragingly. In the course of the month of December the carpenter got the keel of a new vessel laid, and made good progress in cutting the timber and sawing the plank. The two brigs, Maria and Russisloff, were hauled upon the beach and shored up out of the tide's way. They furnished very good accommodations for a large number of the workmen. The Juno remained riding at anchor in the harbor. Watchmen were stationed along the shore, in both directions from the fort, and shouted "All's well," from one end to the other, at intervals, throughout the whole night. All were working cheerfully, and hard enough to kill anybody but Russians. The Indians made us frequent ceremonial visits, and displayed their talent for long speeches and for dancing. They seemed anxious to bury the hatchet, and renew intercourse on friendly terms, which was also the wish of the settlers. In short, everything was in good trim for the winter.

The fare for the present allowed even to the poor workmen was tolerable, as a small portion of the cargo of the Juno was dealt out to them; but the officers had the control of all the luxuries, — if such they may be called; and these, together with the game and fish that were continually brought in, supplied the Governor's table with an abundance of good cheer. There were seven of us who regularly dined at it, and by invitation we frequently had ten.

By the last of the month the weather began to grow cooler; yet, though it was December, we had little or no snow, but much rain and fog. In the forenoon I generally took a stroll along the shore, with my gun, to the place where the new vessel was building. One or two of the officers usually accompanied me; and after reaching the spot we would turn and walk the same distance, about a mile and a half, in the opposite direction. Sometimes we carried home a little game.

January brought cold, but not severe weather. The workmen began to flag. The poor fellows had been driven too hard, regardless of wet and snow. They were now getting sickly, and it was found necessary to ease off their tasks a little. The officers, on the other hand, lived comfortably enough, and even started a new kind of entertainment. The Russians build their log houses in a very substantial manner, of heavy timber, and stop the cracks perfectly tight with moss. Some of them were very large, accommodating after a fashion fifty or sixty persons. Several such were completed just at this time, and it occurred to us that they were well calculated for ball-rooms, and that we could pass away the tedious hours of the night in dancing. We made out bravely in cotillons and contra-dances, but were rather deficient at first in female partners. Many of the under officers had their wives with them, and we picked out some of the Kodiak women, who were accustomed to the Russian dances, and learned the figures easily. When dressed in their finery they appeared quite respectably. His Excellency the Plenipotentiary was always with us on these occasions, and would upon an emergency take the fiddle, on which he was quite a good performer. Dr. Langsdorff and my man Parker took turns at the bow, and with plenty of good resin for the stomach as well as the bow, we made "a gay season" of it.

In February the weather was rather more severe than the previous month, but by no means so cold as in the United States, latitude 42°. The harbors and inlets about the sound were free from ice. With all our attempts to get up amusements, the time hung heavily upon our hands, and we did little else than sleep and long for spring. The Sitcha Indians brought in excellent fresh halibut, which they exchanged for fish-hooks and old clothes. To me especially they were very friendly, and came often to my lodgings, seeming to know that I was not one of the Russians.

The waters of the neighborhood abounded with numerous and choice varieties of the finny tribe, which could be taken at all seasons of the year. The poor Russians might have fared much better than they did, had they been spared from their work to catch them. Labor and exposure began to tell on them. The scurvy had killed a number of them, and many were sick. Dr. Langsdorff frequently remonstrated in their behalf, but to little purpose.

There had been much talk of late among the higher officers upon the expediency of making an expedition to California, with a view to obtaining a fresh supply of provisions, and opening, if possible, a traffic with the Spanish Mission at San Francisco. By the first of March this enterprise was resolved upon and well matured, and active preparations were made to put it into immediate execution. His Excellency, Baron von Resanoff, decided to take charge of it in person. This arrangement gave me some uneasiness, lest he should not return in time to fulfil his promise to proceed with me in May in the Juno to Ochotsk. I explained to him how great the disappointment and inconvenience would be, if my departure was delayed until late in the season. But he silenced my complaints by assuring me that he had ordered the brig Maria, Captain Maschin, to be ready to sail for Ochotsk as soon as the season would permit. With this promise I was constrained to be satisfied. By the active exertion of Lieutenants Schwostoff and Davidoff the

Juno was quickly put in sailing trim, and weighed anchor on the 8th of March for San Francisco. I was invited to accompany them, but declined. Deprived of my friends and companions, I occupied myself, as best I could, in making excursions in baidarkas about the shores and harbors.

Among the domestic animals of the village — and the number was very limited, there being two old cows, eight or ten hogs, and as many dogs — there were two sheep, a buck and a ewe, which I had presented to the Governor on my first visit. The ewe in the course of the winter had been devoured by the wolves or the bears, as it was said; but I thought it more probable by some of the half-starved Russians. The buck became quite a pet with the settlers. Towards spring he began to take advantage of familiar treatment, and show many positive signs of a pugnacious disposition, and with very little respect for persons. As Billy and I were from the same country town, and appeared to be alone among strangers, I always made it a point, when I passed him, to salute him with the familiar phrase of "How are you, Billy?" and he would seem to respond by a look of recognition. It so happened, however, that one day, as I was coming from the Governor's house upon the hill, after a good substantial dinner, and had reached the beginning of the descent where stood the sentinel with Billy at a little distance from him, I gave him the usual greeting, and began to go down, when, perfectly unconscious of having offended man or beast, I received a contusion in the rear, which sent me head-foremost down the declivity with telegraphic velocity, and with a shock which seemed to disturb my whole stowage, even to the very ground tier. I got up as soon as I could collect my scattered senses, and brushed the dust out of my eyes, when looking up the hill I saw Billy, the ram, from whom I had received the assault, making significant demonstrations of another onslaught. I had scarcely scrambled a little to one side before he came down again full charge. This time I dodged him, and, not meeting the check he expected, he went a considerable distance before he could recover himself. Still unsatisfied with the result, he was preparing to make another bolt up hill at me; but now, having the advantage of the ground, I was ready to receive him. The current was this time against him, and his headway a good deal impeded. I caught him by the neck and beat him, and endeavored to turn him off; but as soon as I let him go, he rushed upon me again. Finally, finding it impossible to get rid of him, I took a stone to increase the solidity of my fist, with which I was obliged to pound the creature till the blood ran freely. There was still no yield in him. The sentinel, who had till now been looking on, — to see fair play, I suppose, — seeing that I should probably kill him, left his post and came to the rescue. Thus ended the farcical scene of a battle between a sheep and a Wolf, in which neither could rightfully claim the victory.

April came, and no movement was made towards getting the Maria off the beach, preparatory to the voyage to Ochotsk. Captain Maschin complained that he could not get men. In fact, there was so much work to be done at the settlement, and the number of hands so much reduced by the California expedition, that it was impossible to spare laborers for the vessels. Moreover, many of them were sick, and among the healthy there were no sailors; so operations in the navigation line were suspended.

May commenced with quite pleasant and warm weather. About the 10th, the ship Okain, Captain Jonathan Winship, arrived at the sound. He came direct from the United States without any cargo, but for the express purpose of obtaining Kodiak Indians and baidarkas for a voyage to California to catch sea-otter, on the same plan I had relinquished on the sale of my ship. He made all the necessary arrangements, and sailed about the middle of the month.

The mild weather melted the snow very fast, and by the last of May the frost was all out of the ground. Governor Baranoff was desirous of having a good kitchen garden, and so, to commence the business with a sort of flourish, we made up a pretty substantial picnic party. A little way back from the shore we found a considerable clearing without underbrush, and here we staked out about two acres of land. It was good soil, deep and rich, and we all tried our hand at the spade. The Governor setting the example, we went to work with a good will. Soon getting tired, we adjourned to the refreshments, at which it was thought we showed more talent than at the spade. Some of us, they told us, got quite *blue* by the time we had finished our labors. This was the first ground ever broken for a garden at New Archangel. Another diversion was taking salmon, which at this season ran up into the creeks and inlets in great numbers. As many of the people as could be detached from their regular occupations were set to catching them, and curing them for winter provisions, in the manner I have before described.

While waiting impatiently for the arrival of the Juno, I made many excursions about the sound in my baidarka. About seven or eight miles from the village, there was a hot-water spring which I visited. Situated in a beautiful, romantic place, the water runs down from the foot of a high mountain, in a small serpentine rivulet, for several hundred yards, and empties into a broad basin, several rods in diameter, which has a sandy bottom. The heat of the water at its source is about 150°, and as it spreads over the basin below it cools down to 100°. It is strongly impregnated with sulphur, and with salt and magnesia.

To our great joy, on the 21st of June the Juno returned from California, with all our friends and a tolerable supply of wheat, jerked beef, English beans, &c.; but his Excellency failed to make any arrangement for the future. The Governor of San Francisco remonstrated against sending Russian subjects to hunt sea-otter on the shores and in the harbors of New Albion, and prevailed upon Baron von Resanoff to promise to put a stop to all adventures of that nature.

I immediately applied to Resanoff to know

how and when he intended to fulfil his promise of providing me a passage to Ochotsk. It was now the last of June, and there were no preparations in either of the vessels for that purpose. He told me that the Juno should be got ready as soon as the little vessel could be rigged to accompany her; but the little vessel was yet on the stocks, and it did not appear to me, from the rate at which the work was progressing, that she would be in sailing order before August. In fact, I became quite alarmed, lest the season should be so far advanced that I should be obliged to make a winter journey across the Russian Empire. I had had some conversation with Dr. Langsdorff about taking the brig Russisloff, if they would allow me, and making my own way to Ochotsk. The Doctor eagerly caught at the idea, and resolved to go with me, if I could obtain her. I accordingly made the proposal to his Excellency, and it was readily accepted. He offered to put as many men to work upon the Russisloff as I needed. She was a little craft of twenty-five tons burden, built by the Russian American Company at Bhering's Bay, and in construction a kind of nondescript. She was lying high and dry upon the beach, but, with the assistance rendered, I had her ready for sea in less than a week, well stored with a plenty of the best provisions the place afforded. My crew consisted of seven men, three of whom were Indians and natives of Alashka, making with Dr. Langsdorff, my man Parker, and myself, ten in all. I am happy to say that everything was done by the authorities to expedite my departure, and they all seemed anxious to show me every kindness and attention in their power. Having been furnished with the necessary papers for my voyage, I took leave of his Excellency Baron von Resanoff, Governor Baranoff, and my other friends, and put to sea on the 30th of June, 1806, shaping my course for the island of Kodiak.

V.

Dull Sailing. — I touch at Kodiak and Alashka. — Take in Passengers at Oonalashka. — No Prospect of completing my Voyage this Season. — Determine to winter at Petropowlowsk.

Being at sea again, and on my own vessel, I had leisure for a more deliberate view of the step I had taken, in attempting to seek my own way to Ochotsk, in preference to waiting for the Juno. My little craft was large and safe enough for the purpose; but I was now convinced by her sluggish motion that it was very doubtful whether I gained the port of my destination before it was too late in the autumn to pursue my journey across Siberia. Our best sailing before the wind was hardly five knots, and by the wind two and a half. We had a voyage of 2,500 miles before us, and at a season of the year in that water most subject to calms, light winds, and fogs.

This tract of ocean, from longitude 130° west, along the entire coast of Alashka and through the seas of Kamtchatka and Ochotsk, was at that time the great place of resort of the right whale.

Persecuted in all its other haunts, it had sought refuge in this northern region, where as yet a whale-ship had never made its appearance. We were frequently surrounded by them. Sometimes they would take a position at the windward, and come down towards us, as if they were determined to sink us; but when they had approached within eight or ten rods, they would dip and go under, or make a circuit round us. Most of them were much longer than our vessel, and it would have taken but a slight blow from one to have smashed her into a thousand pieces.

On the 13th of July we saw the high land near the entrance of Cook's Inlet; and on the 17th arrived at the harbor of St. Paul, in the island of Kodiak, after a passage of eighteen days, and which might have been performed by an ordinary sailing craft, with the same winds, in ten days. Here my letters of introduction made me acquainted with Mr. Bander, the Company's Superintendent. He received us with great cordiality, and readily procured me a man to serve as mate. He likewise furnished all the supplies we were in need of, and saw that they were put on board; so that Dr. Langsdorff and myself had little else to do than to look about and see the lions. The village consisted of about forty houses, of various descriptions, including a church, school-house, storehouse, and barracks. The school-house was quite a respectable establishment, well filled with pupils, under the especial care, as teacher, of the "Pope," or ecclesiastic. He instructed them in reading, writing, arithmetic, and keeping accounts. Many among them were excellent scholars in these branches. The Doctor and myself made an excursion to an adjacent island, where the Pope had a considerable tract of land under cultivation, raising potatoes, cabbages, turnips, cucumbers, and other vegetables. He also kept several milch cows, and appeared to live in quite a farmer-like style. We concluded to pass the night with him, and were hospitably entertained by his wife.

Having taken on board some freight of skins and sea-elephant's teeth for Ochotsk, and a cask of brandy for the island of Oonalashka, on the 23d of July we took leave of our friends, Mr. Bander and the Pope, and started again on our route. The wind was so strong from the southeast that I found it impossible to weather the southern point of the island, and thus to get to the westward of it. I concluded to bear up, and pass through the Schelikoff's Strait. This is a channel formed by an archipelago of islands (of which

Kodiak is the principal), and the peninsula of Alashka. But by reason of light and contrary winds, we did not get fairly into the strait until the 26th, and shortly after encountered a strong wind from the west, with heavy squalls, which soon increased to such a severe gale, that we were compelled to seek shelter on the Alashka shore. Here I found my Indian sailors, who had proved good men from the beginning, to be of the greatest service. I mentioned above that they were natives of Alashka, and they were perfectly acquainted with the shore. They pointed out to me a good harbor, for which I steered; and as we rounded the point at its entrance, which was called Kudak, a baidarka containing one man came alongside. He turned out to be the father of one of my sailors, and they had not seen each other before for two years. They did not appear, however, to be over-rejoiced at this accidental meeting. They embraced each other after the Russian custom, had a little chat together, and then went about their business, without showing any disposition for further communication.

In the course of the night the gale increased so much that I deemed it prudent to let go our best bow-anchor; but with the return of light the wind abated, and the weather became quite pleasant. Doctor Langsdorff and myself took our baidarka, and went to the village, which was situated on the opposite side of the harbor from where we lay. It consisted of eight or ten habitations, which looked more like mounds of earth than houses. They contained but one room, of an oval form, and about fifteen feet across. The earth was dug out about three feet in depth, and raised from the surface about three feet more, and to enter we had to crawl on our hands and knees. The light was admitted through windows of transparent skins, as a substitute for glass. Their quarters were certainly comfortable for winter. The floors were covered with spruce boughs, and mats were laid over them, which made the apartment dry and warm. An aperture was left in the top for ventilation. The outside was covered with a luxurious growth of grass. The occupants were principally women, with a few old men; the young men had all gone out hunting the sea-otter, in the Russian service. Those at home seemed to be quite happy and contented, and were all employed in making water-proof garments from the entrails of sea-lions, for their husbands and sweethearts. We bought of them a number of articles of their manufacture, —

curious and very neat work,— such as pocket-books, baskets, &c., — and paid them in tobacco and beads.

On the 28th of July, the wind being moderate and favorable, we put to sea again, and pursued our course to the westward along the coast of Alashka. We made but slow progress on our voyage, and by the 9th of August we had only reached the end of the peninsula. The same day we passed through between the island of Oonemak and the easternmost of the Fox Islands. On the 12th we arrived at the island of Oonalashka. I had no cause to stop here beyond the desire of replenishing our water-casks and stores. Owing to our tardy progress,— having as yet, performed only one third of the distance from Kodiak to Ochotsk,— our provisions were more than half consumed. I therefore felt myself constrained to put in for a further supply.

The Company's Superintendent, Lariwanoff, a gentleman highly esteemed by them, had died a short time previous to our arrival, leaving a widow and an only child, a daughter about eighteen years of age. I was received by his successor with much kindness, and with an apparent disposition to facilitate my voyage. The harbor, Illuluk, was spacious and well sheltered on all sides. There was a good anchorage in four or five fathoms of water, on a sand and clay bottom, at a convenient distance from the shore. While making some necessary repairs on my little vessel, and getting supplies aboard, Madam Lariwanoff learned that I was bound to Ochotsk. She immediately came, and on her knees entreated me to have compassion on her lonely and bereaved condition, and let her and her daughter take passage with me. Irkutsk in Siberia was her native place, and thither she was desirous of returning after a residence on this island ten years. Her solicitations were so earnest that I had not the heart to refuse her, and notwithstanding our contracted accommodations, entirely unfit for a woman's occupation, I resolved to take her under my protection. I went aboard, and set about making the best possible arrangements for her comfort, gave up my bunk, enlarged it sufficiently for the mother and child together, and partitioned off the little cabin with a canvas screen. I immediately commenced taking on board their goods and chattels, with which, however, they were not overburdened; but she had been preparing to leave the island for some time, and had accumulated a goodly stock of provisions of various kinds, —

several barrels of eggs, put up in oil, smoked geese in abundance, dried and pickled fish of an excellent quality, and other things equally good. Thus our fare promised to be the best the island afforded. In the mean time the Superintendent began to make objections, and throw difficulties in the way of the old lady's going with me. She might make reports which would not redound to his credit. But I had it in my power to silence all his objections, having on board the cask of brandy, which it was at my option to leave with him, or take to Ochotsk. On his application for it, I demurred until he withdrew all his opposition to the widow's leaving, and was willing to grant anything on the island we wished. He was a dear lover of " the ardent."

Everything now went on smoothly, and in a few days we were ready for sea; but adverse winds detained us, and I seized the opportunity to take a stroll over the island with the Doctor and Superintendent. It was totally bare of trees and shrubs, and with little or no game but foxes. The whole value and importance of the Aleutian group consist in the sea animals taken on their shores and bays, such as fur-seals, walruses, sea-lions, and sea-otter; though of the latter there were few. This is likewise the principal depot of the fisheries of the smaller islands, and from here the furs are periodically shipped to Ochotsk. In the course of our ramble we ascended some high table-land with the hope of obtaining a view of the new island, which we were informed had recently made its appearance in the Sea of Kamtchatka, to the northwest of Oonalashka; but we were disappointed by a thick mist's setting in, which obscured all distant objects. After wandering about in the numerous fox-paths, and with great caution, to avoid the many traps set for those animals, we returned to the village, somewhat hungry and leg-weary, and with but little satisfaction to boast of, beyond traversing a region rendered classic by the verse of Campbell, in the "Pleasures of Hope": —

> "Now far he sweeps, where scarce a summer smiles,
> On Behring's rocks, or Greenland's naked isles;
> Cold on his midnight watch the breezes blow,
> From wastes that slumber in eternal snow;
> And waft, across the waves' tumultuous roar,
> The wolf's long howl from Oonalashka's shore."

But, in fact, I was the only Wolf ever known upon the island. Nevertheless, I came near verifying the poet's language, as I barely escaped being caught in one of those fox-traps; in which event I should have probably howled lustily, for they were terrible instruments.

August 16th, the wind and weather being favorable, Madame Lariwanoff, her daughter, and man-servant, came on board, and we put to sea; and I have every reason to believe with the fervent prayers of every individual upon the island for God's blessing upon their patroness, and good speed to our little craft. The next day we saw the new island, to which I was desirous to get near enough to send a baidarka, particularly as the Doctor was anxious to get some specimens of natural history; but a thick fog coming up, and having a leading wind, we concluded to continue our voyage without loss of time. On the 18th we lost sight of the islands, and, with a light wind and rain, slowly pursued our course to the westward, across the Sea of Kamtchatka, to the north of the Aleutian group; but such was our tardy progress, that by the 28th we had only reached the neighborhood of Atter, the most western island. Then for ten days in succession we had calms, fogs, and light adverse winds. Our patience was sorely tried, but the monotony of our life was alleviated by the numerous and great variety of sea-birds, which were constantly flying round us, and furnished endless sport with the musket. And here I feel bound to record the marvellous skill, or good luck, of the Doctor, as he killed a whole flock of four wild geese at one shot; and, what was still better, we got out our baidarka, and took them all aboard.

Still creeping along with the same dull winds and disagreeable weather, on the 3d of September we found ourselves in latitude 52° north, and longitude 170° east, which placed us a considerable distance southwest of Atter. We began to entertain fears lest we should not reach the port of our destination in season; but on the 6th, for the first time since leaving Oonalashka, we took a strong northeast gale, which carried us into the vicinity of the Kurile Islands. Our hopes began to revive, and the prospect of reaching Ochotsk to brighten; but again were we doomed to disappointment. A severe blow from the southeast obliged us to heave to, with a heavy sea running; and we drifted back over the course we had just sailed, at the rate of two miles an hour. A considerable quantity of the provisions for the sailors consisted of whale's blubber, which was hanging on our quarter, and was of course well soaked with oil. This we found to be a great advantage, for it made a "slick" to the windward for nearly a mile, and prevented the sea from breaking over us.

Strong westerly winds continued to baffle us until the 14th, when, having no hope of reaching Ochotsk before the autumn was so far spent that we should be obliged to make a winter's journey across Siberia, we concluded to alter our course, and sail for the harbor of St. Peter and St. Paul, or Petropowlowsk, in Kamtchatka. We made port on the 22d, and anchored abreast the village. We were kindly and hospitably received by the Company's Superintendent, as well as by the officers of the military department, and especially by Major Antony Ivanah and lady, who showed me many civilities. Madam Lariwanoff and daughter were taken in charge by the Superintendent, and provided with comfortable quarters. The Doctor and myself at once took temporary lodgings on the shore, until we could make permanent arrangements for the winter. Having discharged all the cargo, and dismantled our little craft, we hauled her up on the beach at the first spring tide. Provisions and accommodations were provided at the settlement for the crew as well as ourselves; and in fact the people seemed desirous to do everything in their power to render our stay amongst them as comfortable and agreeable as the nature of the place would admit.

VI.

SETTLED FOR ANOTHER WINTER.—ARRIVAL OF OLD FRIENDS.—DOGS AND SLEDGING.—A RUSSIAN CHRISTENING.

DETAINED for another winter, we endeavored at once to make the acquaintance of the inhabitants of the village, and to become familiar with the country in its vicinity. We were introduced to all the people of note, and kindly entertained by them. We made pedestrian excursions for several miles in every direction, and visited all the common places of resort. The scenery was picturesque, and the view from the elevations was beautiful and grand. The Awatska Bay, or outer harbor, as it is called, is completely land-locked, and at the same time so extensive, that a thousand ships might ride at anchor in it with safety. The distant mountains, and particularly the high peak Awatska, add greatly to the landscape. The latter presents the imposing spectacle of a volcano in full blast, always overhung with a cloud of smoke, and constantly belching fire and lava.

We had only one source of annoyance at the village during the early part of our stay, and we soon became well used to that. I refer to the barking of the numerous dogs, though it can scarcely be called barking, for they howl like a wolf. At sunset regularly they would begin their serenade at one end of the settlement, — which, by the way, extended all round the harbor, — and in the course of half an hour all the voices would join in the chorus, and keep it up all night long. With this single temporary drawback, we passed our time very pleasantly until the first of November. By then we had visited on foot all the places in the more immediate neighborhood, and we concluded to make a short boat excursion to a small river named Paratunka, to see some warm springs situated several miles from its mouth. This spring issues from the ground in a boiling state, and spreads out over a basin excavated for its reception. It forms an excellent bathing-place, being of suitable depth, with a sandy bottom, and the bather can choose any degree of warmth he pleases. The water is impregnated with sulphur and other minerals. We found here some Russian invalids who had come to enjoy the use of the spring. All the rivers in the neighborhood abounded in salmon, though it was so late in the season; and we protracted our stay for a day or two, hunting and fishing, and boiling our game in the hot water of the spring.

On our return to the village we were surprised to find one of our old Norfolk Sound friends, Lieutenant Davidoff, who had arrived at the harbor in command of the little new vessel built at Sitcha, and called the Awos. He had left the Sound in August, accompanied by the Juno, under the command of Lieutenant Schwostoff, and having Baron von Resanoff on board to be carried to Ochotsk. He had parted with them off the Kurile Islands. About the middle of November Lieutenant Schwostoff made his appearance with the Juno. After landing his Excellency about Ochotsk, he received orders to proceed to one of the southernmost of the Kurile Islands, and break up a Japanese settlement reported to have been established there. He found at the place four Japanese, with a large stock of goods for trade with the islanders, consisting of rice, tobacco, fish-nets, lacquered ware, salt, cotton, silk, and many other articles; all of which he seized without opposition, and brought Japanese, goods, and all to Kamtchatka. Thus we met our old friends in a very unexpected manner.

As we were doomed to pass another winter in this region, their company was very pleasant, and to have the Juno in sight again was especially agreeable to me.

I now took lodgings in a shanty owned and occupied by a very clever old man, named Andra, and his wife and little boy. I called him in a familiar way Starruk, that is old man, and his wife Starruke, old woman. He was quite thrifty for the place, and was one of the few in the village who owned and kept a cow. This was a fortunate circumstance, for good milk was a rarity in that section. His shanty was warm and comfortable, and was divided into three apartments. In one corner of the largest they made a bunk for me, and curtained it round. My man Parker slept in the same room on a movable bed. In the next room, which was the cooking-room, there was a large brick oven, or furnace, and on the top of this slept Starruk, his wife, and little boy. The third apartment was devoted to the cow and her fodder. At this place I took my meals at night and morning, but dined by general invitation at the Company's table, at the house of the Superintendent. Comfortably settled in my new quarters, I prepared for a long winter's siege.

It was necessary to be provided with a set of good dogs and a sledge. With the assistance of Starruk I was soon possessed of five of the best animals of the kind, and had them tied up near the house, that they might get accustomed to me, and be ready for use. In the spring of the year the dogs are turned loose, and left to provide for themselves, in the best way they can. Hence they are great thieves until the herring season comes, when they have an abundant supply of food, which they go into the water and catch for themselves, until they become very fat, and unfit for use. At that season, too, great quantities of the herring are caught by the owners of the dogs, and split and dried in the sun, to feed them in the winter, when they give them nothing else.

I also purchased a first-rate sledge, at once light and handsome, fur garments, Kamtchatka boots, bear-skin, and everything needed to make my equipage complete; and, now fully prepared, I waited impatiently for the snow. There had been already several squalls, but about the last of November the ground was well covered and the winter set in. My dogs were in good travelling condition, and I now made my first essay, with three of them to begin with. The style in which they tumbled me about in the snow was "a caution," as Paddy says, and furnished great amusement to the villagers. But I persevered, with a determination to make myself master of the business, and at the end of a week was quite an adroit performer. The sledges were so constructed, that it required nearly as much skill and practice to keep in equilibrium as in skating; but when well understood, they afforded a most splendid recreation and agreeable exercise. Being soon able to harness and manage my five dogs with dexterity, we used frequently to make a party, consisting of Langsdorff, Schwostoff, Davidoff, and Miasnikoff, and go out on excursions to the neighboring villages, from ten to twenty miles distant. When the weather was unfavorable, we had balls and parties; and in this way the weeks and months of the long winter passed off quite cheerfully.

About the 1st of January, 1807, the Governor-General, Koscheleff, who resides at Nischney, which is the capital of Kamtchatka, made his annual visit of inspection to all the military posts on the peninsula. His entrance into Petropowlowsk with a long handsome sledge, a Kamtchadale on each side, as conductors, and a string of twenty dogs, was quite a new and pleasing sight to me. During his stay of five days, we had royal feastings and visitings; and when he left, half the village accompanied him to the distance of ten or fifteen miles, myself among the number. We made a string nearly a mile long.

The sledging in Kamtchatka is not without some adverse casualties to the best of managers. One occurred to me which I will narrate. I was coming from Melka, an interior village, with a load of frozen salmon, in company with my landlord, Starruk, and, my dogs being better than his, I got several miles ahead of him. The snow was deep, but the top was crusted, and the underbrush all covered. The surface was perfectly smooth, but interrupted by numerous large trees; and to avoid them our track was serpentine. At last we came to an inclined plane of a mile or so in length, and, my sledge being heavily laden, it became necessary for me to be constantly on my guard, and keep a sharp lookout. Accordingly I took the usual preliminary precaution in such cases, of sitting sideways, with the left hand hold of the fore part, left foot on the runner, and my right leg extended; my foot, slipping over the snow, operated as a sort of an outrigger. The dogs at the same time, fearful lest the sledge should run on to them, went down the declivity like lightning. The trees seemed to grow thicker and thicker, and to avoid them it soon became hard up and hard down with me. At last, coming to a sharp curve to the right, the sledge, sheering to the other side, struck with such force as to scatter my whole establishment, and I received such a blow on the head that it stunned me, and laid me out on the snow unconscious. When I came to a little, and looked up, I saw my sledge was partly a wreck, four of my dogs had broken from their harness and gone on, while one, left fast in his gear, was sitting on his haunches, and watching me with wonder, as much as if to say, "How came you here?" It was not long before Starruk came up. He asked me what was the matter. I replied, that some one in passing had run foul of me. "No," said he, "I guess you run foul of that tree"; which, on collecting my scattered thoughts, I found to be the fact. But as there were no bones broken, I brightened up, and, with the old man's assistance, caught my dogs again, repaired damages, and pursued my journey, not a little worse for my tumble.

I will mention another circumstance which occurred to me,— not that there was anything extraordinary in it, but merely to show the sagacity of dogs, and the convenience of travelling with them. I was coming from a village about ten miles distant. It was dusk when I started, and night soon closed in with Egyptian darkness and an arctic snow-storm. I could not see even my dogs. The new snow soon covered and obliterated the old track. It was difficult to tell whether I was going ahead or standing still, without putting my foot through the new-fallen snow down to the old crust. In this way I went on for an hour or so, the dogs making very slow progress, and very hard work of it. Not being able to see anything, I somehow or other became persuaded that the dogs had inclined to the left of the beaten track, and consequently I kept urging them to the right. Thus I went on for some time, until I found myself in a forest of large trees, and had much difficulty in keeping clear of them. At last I became decidedly bewildered, but convinced that I had lost my way. Not knowing whither I was going, and fearing that I might wander, the Lord knew where, during the long night, I concluded to halt, and make my dogs fast to a tree. I then sat awhile on my sledge, and listened, to see if I could hear anybody, and finally prepared my bear-skin and fur garments for a night's bivouac. I had not lain more than an hour before I heard the howling of dogs; my own immediately answered them. I found they were approaching, and when I judged them to be within hailing distance, I called out. A man called out in return, and soon drove up. It was a Kamtchadale coming from Petropowlowsk. It appeared that I had urged the dogs a considerable distance from the proper track, which, with the new-comer's assistance, I regained. He told me not to attempt to guide the dogs, but to let them pick their own way. I accordingly sat on my sledge for an hour or so, scarcely realizing that I was moving, till at last I turned my eyes up, and found myself right under the light of my own window.

These little mishaps occurred while I was yet a novice in the art of sledging; but I soon became acquainted with the habits and dispositions of my dogs, and they became accustomed to me, so that I travelled fearlessly, alone or in company, and made excursions to all the villages in the southern part of the peninsula within a hundred miles of Petropowlowsk. While I was amusing myself in the southern, the Doctor was traversing the northern part of Kamtchatka all by himself, and collecting specimens of natural history.

I was always an admirer of the rigid adherence

of the Russians to their religious forms and ceremonies. I never saw a Russian, high' or low, who did not, both before and after eating, ask a blessing, and give thanks to God for his bounty, apparently with a sincere and thankful heart. Yet there are some things very absurd in their ceremonies. For instance, I was invited to the christening of a child at the house of the Superintendent, and requested to stand as godfather with Dr. Langsdorff, as it was necessary, I was told, to have two godfathers and two godmothers. At the appointed time we repaired to the house, where we found the pope and numerous guests already assembled. The pope had brought with him a small box, resembling a tea-caddy, containing, as was said, consecrated oil. A large tub full of water was placed in the centre of the room, and the pope's apparatus near at hand. He then commenced the operation with prayers, after which, he took the child in his arms and plunged it under the water. Then, with a small brush and some oil from the box, he crossed the child all over its body and legs, and afterwards marched round the tub, and we, the godfathers and godmothers, followed, in Indian file, three times round. The child was then given to one of the godfathers, crossed again, and round the tub we went three times more. And so it continued until we all had taken our turns, and made fifteen circuits of the tub. Now I thought this, or the greater part of it, a nonsensical ceremony, and a piece of rigmarole; but it was not my part to find fault or object to it, and I willingly conformed to the custom.

When it was over, the tub taken away, and a table put in its place, madam, the mother of the child, brought on the goodies, pies of flesh and pies of fish, cakes of various kinds, preserved berries, and many other things; but what astounded me most was that a bottle of real ardent spirits found its way to the table on this extra occasion, an article which had disappeared from among our stores several months previous. The pope paid his respects to it with peculiar unction, and a glowing countenance, and the rest of us were not slow in following suit. This was one of the friendly gatherings to which I made it a point never to refuse an invitation; and I found the Russians were very fond of celebrating birthdays, christenings, and as many holidays as they could make an excuse for.

VII.

VOYAGE TO OCHOTSK. — JOURNEY FROM OCHOTSK TO YAKUTSK.

ABOUT the last of March the snow began to disappear rapidly, and by the middle of April the ground was so bare that our sledging parties were abandoned. The ice had left the bay, and all hands were at work, under the directions of Lieut. Schwostoff and Davidoff, sawing and breaking up the ice in the inner harbor, in order to extricate the Juno and Awos, which had been preparing to sail for some time. By the 25th the channel was cleared, and the two vessels put to sea, with the four Japanese who had passed the winter with us. Their destination was the northern Japanese Islands, where they intended to land their passengers, and make some further attempts to establish an intercourse with the people.

By this movement I was prompted to get my little craft afloat and prepare for the remainder of my voyage. I was admonished, by those acquainted with the breaking up of the ice in the rivers at the head of the Ochotsk Sea, not to be in a hurry; but my anxiety to be off rendered me deaf to all remonstrances; and on the 22d of May I was ready. At this point I was beset by a number of persons, both male and female, for a passage to Ochotsk. I concluded to take five in addition to Madam Lariwanoff and daughter, viz. one elderly widow woman, one old woman and her daughter, one very respectable young man in the Company's service, and one other gentleman. Our party now numbered eighteen. We were tolerably well equipped, and had an abundant supply of such provisions as the place afforded. When our arrangements were all completed, Doctor Langsdorff and myself devoted a day to taking leave of the many friends who had entertained us during the winter; and I particularly of my old landlord and landlady, Starruk and Starruke. To the former I paid what he thought a very liberal compensation for the apartment I had occupied at his house. I also made him a present of my sledge, its equipage, and my dogs, with the exception of one, which I took with me.

To Starruke I gave my bedding, curtains, and furniture. I then bade good by to these warm-hearted people, and left them with their warmest prayers for a prosperous voyage. Our passengers now came on board, and, after making the best accommodations for them our contracted quarters would admit, on the 26th, with fair weather, we bade adieu to Petropowlowsk, and weighed anchor.

Favorable winds continued just long enough to give us a good offing, when they became light and adverse, with calms, and so continued for several days. On the 30th, having just taken a brisk breeze, which was driving us along, for a wonder, at nearly five knots, we ran into a large whale which was lying near the surface. We somehow slid up on his back so as to raise our little vessel two or three feet and throw her over on her side four or five streaks. It was like striking a rock, and brought us to a complete stand-still. The monster soon showed himself, gave a spout, "kicked" his flukes and went down. He did not appear to be hurt, nor were we hurt, but most confoundedly frightened. I sounded the pump immediately, and found that all was safe as to leakage, and we continued on our course quite satisfied with the result.

June 3d, we passed through between the second and third Kurile Islands from the southern part of Kamtchatka, and entered the Sea of Ochotsk. Here again we were annoyed by the calms, which continued with but little variance until the 14th, when we had reached latitude 58°. We now began to meet ice, at first so scattered that we thought it possible to push through it; but after working in amongst it for a few hours, it became so compact as to be impassable, and extended east, west, and north as far as the eye could reach, even from the masthead a solid mass. Finding it impossible to proceed any farther, and as the ice was closing rapidly around us, I deemed it advisable to avail myself of that better part of valor, discretion, and pole out as we had poled in; for I had soon discovered that our little craft was too slight to deal freely with heavy ice. Having gained the open water, I steered to the eastward all day without finding any passage-way. The wind proving unfavorable for sailing in that direction, we turned and went westward. Thus we continued for ten days, making various attempts to get clear of the ice, and at last succeeded. On the 26th, at meridian, we found our latitude 59° 20', and the land was in sight. On the 27th, we anchored off the mouth of the river Ochota. At 2 P. M., the tide turned, and we crossed the bar, entered the harbor of Ochotsk, and made fast to the Company's wharf. Thus terminated a long and tedious passage of thirty-three days.

We were told here that the ice had only left the rivers and bays four or five days. We were likewise informed, to our great grief, that his Excellency Baron von Resanoff had died at Krasnojarsk in Siberia, on his route to St. Petersburg. He had fallen from his horse on the road from Ochotsk to Yakutsk, which was supposed to be the cause of his death. The passport and letters I had previously received from his Excellency at once made me acquainted with the Company's Superintendent, Mr. Petroff; likewise with the commandant of the port, Captain Bucharin. By both these gentlemen I was treated with the utmost kindness and civility; and, knowing my desire to be on my way to St. Petersburg, they were both anxious to afford me every facility in their power. A taboo was immediately put upon a sufficient number of the first horses that arrived from Yakutsk. With the greatest possible despatch, it was necessary to wait a few days, and in the mean time I was taken round the place to see the lions. They did not amount to much. The town was situated on a sand spit, washed by the sea on one side and the river Ochota on the other. The river Kuchtin unites with the Ochota near the harbor's mouth, which, at the best, is an indifferent one, and not accessible to vessels drawing more than eight feet of water. The town is joined to the mainland by a narrow neck of marshy ground, which is often inundated. In fact, it appeared to me that any extra rise of the river or sea would swamp the whole place. Some ship-building was going on here, and many convicts were employed in the government service.

For my convenience, the privilege was accorded to me by the Company of selecting a Russian subject to accompany me on my road, as a kind of an assistant. A young man by the name of Kutsnetsoff, or Smith, was pointed out as one desirous of going with me, but the Superintendent did not feel authorized to release him from the service, unless I should think proper to select him, and I accordingly did so. He had been ten years at the settlements on the Aleutian Islands, and was anxious to return to Irkutsk, his native place. He had a brother in Moscow, a merchant of high standing, who was at the head of the Company's establishment there.

On the morning of July 3d, my horses, eleven in number, were brought out. They did not look very promising, as they had been overworked on the route hither. This was rather discouraging, for it was important that they should be in a good condition for a journey of 500 miles, through a country with no signs of a settlement except a few log shanties at great distances asunder, and no road but a serpentine footpath; moreover, we had a fair amount of luggage, and for comfort and convenience we were obliged to carry a tent, cooking-utensils, and bear-skins, &c. for bedding. Bad as they were, these horses were better than none, and I must make the best of them.

Having completed my preparations, I took leave of my highly esteemed friend, Dr. Langsdorff, who intended to remain a week or so for the promotion of his favorite object; also of Madam Lariwanoff and her daughter, my other passengers, and sailors,— particularly of the three Alashka Indians, who had proved themselves excellent men, and rendered me good service. They fell upon their knees and entreated me to take them with me. As this was impracticable,

I could only make them a gratuity in rubles, and recommend them to the kindness of Mr. Petroff, in whose employ and charge they were. Having finished our leave-takings, we mounted our horses. There were five of us,— myself and two aids, Parker and Kutsnetsoff, and two Yakutas, the owners of the horses, and acting as guides. Three of the other six horses carried our luggage, and the remaining three were kept in reserve for a change on the road. Dr. Langsdorff, the Superintendent, Captain Bucharin, and other friends, accompanied us to the outskirts of the town to take another and a final farewell, and we then put spurs to our horses, and struck into the woods. We went on at quite a spirited pace until five o'clock, when we arrived at a small clearing called Medwescha Golowa, or Bear's Head, where there were a few huts. Here we dismounted to lunch, and rest our horses for half an hour; and then resumed our journey. At seven in the evening we pitched our tent, and camped for the night, in a good place for our horses to graze. As we carried no provender, this was a matter of great importance throughout our whole journey. We turned our beasts loose, and the Yakutschians watched them by turns through the night. The distance we travelled this day since eleven o'clock was 45 versts.*

Ochotsk is situated in latitude 59° 30', and Yakutsk in about 63°. The direction of our course was west-northwest and the distance in a bee-line 500 miles; but by reason of the tortuous nature of the route we were obliged to pursue, the distance was much increased. In such an extent of wild country there were doubtless many objects that would have attracted the attention of the man of science; but being myself neither naturalist, botanist, nor geologist, I had no call to search to the right or to the left for specimens. My business was to push on as fast as my horses could carry me, having an especial regard for my bills of exchange. I paid but little attention to the names of the numerous small rivers and mountains which we crossed, merely noticing some of the principal. To me the country wore even a greater degree of sameness than other unsettled regions.

July 4th. We collected our horses and struck our tent at 7 A. M., mounted, and continued our journey. Several large caravans of horses

---

* A verst is 212¼ rods, or, roughly, five eighths of a mile.

passed us in the forenoon, laden with flour and provisions for Ochotsk. In the afternoon, we crossed a ridge of tolerably high mountains, and then came upon swampy ground. At five o'clock we reached a small river; but it was so deep we were obliged to ferry our luggage over in a boat, and swim our horses. We went on until eight in the evening, when we encamped. The distance travelled this day was 47 versts.

July 5th. We had a thick fog and rain through the night. It cleared up in the morning, and we mounted at seven, and continued our journey through valleys and over mountains, with extremely bad travelling, the whole day. The weather growing hot, we were sorely annoyed by the mosquitos, and were obliged to wear leather gloves and a kind of hood in the shape of a sun-bonnet, with a gauze veil to protect the face. Our white horses became perfectly pink with the blood drawn from them by these insects. We pitched our tents at six in the evening. The distance travelled this day was 55 versts.

July 6th. Started at seven, and had pleasant, but rather warm weather. In the course of the day we forded several small rivers without unpacking our horses, and passed four caravans with stores for Ochotsk. At five in the afternoon we came to a small group of shanties where was kept a magazine of provisions and a stud of horses for government emergencies. This place was 190 versts from Ochotsk. Taking tea here, we proceeded until seven o'clock, and then encamped in a tolerably good grazing-place. The distance travelled this day was 55 versts.

July 7th. Started this morning at six. The travelling was extremely bad, and the ground swampy; the horses sank in the mire up to their saddle-girths. By noon we came to better going. Passed to-day, beside caravans, several droves of cattle on the way to Ochotsk. Distance, 60 versts.

July 8th. Fine weather, but the travelling very poor again. At ten in the morning arrived at the banks of the river Allacjun, one of the largest tributaries of the Aldan. We ferried our baggage across, and swam our horses. At three in the afternoon we halted and turned our beasts out to graze. Owing to the uneven and miry road they had passed over, they were very much fatigued and galled. Distance this day, 40 versts.

July 9th. Started at six in the morning. Passed several caravans, and at five in the afternoon met the government post for Ochotsk. At nine, pitched our tent on the bank of a small tributary of the Allacjun. Distance this day, 65 versts.

July 10th. Rained all the fore part of the day. Our route was through a gorge between high ridges of mountains. Distance travelled, 50 versts.

July 11th. The weather was pleasant and warm, the country rugged and mountainous. At four in the afternoon we came to the foot of a high and steep mountain, and halted to make preparations for the ascent. Our horses had already become so weak and travel-worn, that it was doubtful whether they would succeed in crossing it. My Yakutschian guides lifted their tails to ascertain their strength. On those that had limber tails the weight of the baggage was reduced, and increased on those that had stiff tails. I noticed them also pulling hair from the manes, and tying it to the branches of trees; whether this was done to invoke the good, or propitiate the evil spirits, I could not make out. After they had adjusted things to suit them, we took off our coats, and started, leading our beasts. The ground was so very springy that it was with great difficulty that we could pick our way. Two of the baggage horses mired before we reached the top, and we were obliged to unload in order to extricate them. We finally gained the summit, — which after all was not so very high, — and, having rested a little, descended. Continuing our course through a narrow valley, at 6 P. M. we crossed the river Allakum, and stopped at a small cluster of shanties on its left bank. There was a ferry for bipeds, but such of the poor horses as were able were obliged to swim. The stream was so rapid, that mine had a hard tug to get across. Distance this day, 50 versts.

It was necessary to make a halt soon for a day or two to recruit, and this was a favorable place. The government had a station and postilion here. Four of my horses were completely broken down, and I left them, and hired six fresh ones. We also replenished our stock of provisions.

July 14th. Mounted at 5 A. M., and passed over a very high mountain, and descended into a narrow, serpentine valley, in which we travelled the better part of the day. We passed several caravans and droves of beef cattle. Distance, 55 versts.

July 15th. Our route this day over boggy ground again, and the travelling was therefore as poor as ever. Our horses' backs were very sore, and they were all nearly exhausted. We pitched our tent early in the afternoon at a good grazing-place, to give them a little rest. Distance, 40 versts.

July 16th. The weather this day was warm and pleasant, and road not so mountainous as it had been. At 5 P. M., one of our horses gave out, and we left him. Continuing on until seven, we pitched our tent on the banks of the White River. Distance, 50 versts.

July 17th. At 6 A. M. we mustered together our horses, and found that four were missing. We spent half the day in a fruitless search for them, and then concluded that they were either killed or frightened away by the bears, which are very plentiful in this region. We pursued our journey, much of the way through mud and water up to the saddle-girths. Distance, 30 versts.

July 18th. Struck our tent at 7 A. M., and at nine crossed the White River. All the early part of the day, until within twenty versts of the Aldan, we found the road very good. Here we saw before us an extensive morass, to avoid which it would be necessary to go the distance of thirty versts. This morass was about a quarter of a mile in breadth, and partially covered with water, interspersed with little grass knolls, which were soft and unsteady. Disagreeable as the prospect was, we concluded to go straight across. We accordingly fastened on the baggage tighter, stripped off all our clothes but shirt and pants, and secured them to the saddles, and started, leading our horses, each one picking out the way for himself. In about half an hour we succeeded in flouncing through without accident; but it was a tiresome job, and we got well plastered with mud. Putting ourselves and luggage in order, we proceeded until 10 P. M., when we reached the government station on the right bank of the Aldan, having left two of our horses on the road exhausted.

We had now reached the principal station on the route, which was about two thirds the distance to Yakutsk; and I determined to halt for a day or two to recruit, after passing fifteen in the saddle. At first I was quite pleased with the idea of this land excursion, but I found in a very little while that it was no joke. I was sore all over, from head to foot. The clumsy saddles we rode upon were anything but convenient. The pommels were of wood and raised about six inches, and in the hollow between sat the rider. There was just space enough for an ordinary-sized man; and being myself light and spare of person, there was plenty of room for me to shake in my seat. I soon hit upon an expedient, however, to alleviate my suffering. I bolstered up with pillows, so that by the fourth day my pains and aches subsided, and afterward I was tolerably comfortable. Still the incessant torments of the mosquitos and miry roads were hard to bear. I soon grew sick of this horse-marine navigation, and came to the conclusion that the spray of the sea was far preferable to a mud bath. We made up as well as we could for the annoyance of bad roads, bogs, and small rivers, by taking reasonable care of the inner man. I mentioned before, that we took our cooking apparatus and provisions with us. We had bread and sugar, and the tea-kettle was in constant requisition morning and evening. Sometimes at the shanties on the route we obtained a little milk. At noon we generally had a substantial lunch of Bologna sausage or corned meat, and a glass of schnapps.

Having rested and refreshed ourselves sufficiently, I made an arrangement with the postilion of the station to take us through the remainder of the distance, as from here to the banks of the Lena there were relays of horses at points twenty-five or thirty versts asunder.

July 21st. Being all ready for a move, our horses were gathered together at the river's side. There was only one small boat belonging to the place, in which we made out to ferry ourselves and baggage over; but the poor horses were obliged to swim. Such was their dislike to the water, that we were detained half a day trying to force them in. At last we succeeded, by taking two of them by the halter, one on each side of the boat, and letting the others, five in number, follow on their own hook. The current was so rapid that they swam the distance of two versts, when the width of the stream at this point was only one, before they reached the opposite shore. They crawled up on the bank quite exhausted, and we were obliged to remain awhile for them to recover. At 2 P. M. we mounted and pursued our journey. At eight in the evening we pitched our tent at the first post-station after leaving the Aldan. The distance travelled was 35 versts.

July 22d. Changed horses and started at 6 A. M. The travelling was much improved, and at 5 P. M. we came to the second stand, on the bank of the Anger, after a ride of 50 versts. We passed over this river in the usual manner, and went on 25 versts more to the third station, where we paused for the night, quite satisfied with our day's progress.

July 23d. At 9 A. M. started with fresh horses and continued on our route. The travelling was still more improved, and the country generally had a more agreeable appearance. The high mountains had disappeared, and we rode over level prairies, beautifully diversified with grasses and a great variety and profusion of flowers. Among the latter the red pink predominated, the odor of which scented the whole atmosphere, and made the journey delightful. At 1 P. M. we changed our horses at the fourth station, and at six arrived at the fifth, where we passed the night. Distance, 60 versts.

July 24th. We had pleasant weather, and at 7 A. M. started on our route. At 8 P. M. we arrived at the seventh station, where we encamped for the night, and paid the postilion 35 rubles for the use of his horses, this being the last station to which he had authority to take us. Distance, 60 versts.

July 25th. At 7 A. M. we resumed our

journey under the charge of another postilion. Our horses, since leaving the Aldan, had generally been very good; but this morning I found myself on a splendid animal, of a cream color, singularly and beautifully marked. A dark brown stripe about a hand's breadth ran from the crupper to the withers, and then spread over the shoulders in a broad patch; his mane and tail reached nearly to the ground. I could see that he was well groomed and cared for, but I was rather shy about mounting him at first. I was assured, however, that he was well broken and gentle, and I found him so. He was certainly the most perfect creature of the kind I ever rode or set eyes on. The plains over which we travelled this day were dotted over with innumerable cattle and horses grazing. At 9 P. M. we arrived at the tenth station and pitched our tent. Distance, 75 versts.

July 26th. At 7 A. M. we continued on our route, and at 4 P. M. reached the right bank of the river Lena, which I crossed, and was kindly received and entertained at the Company's establishment at Yakutsk. This town, the capital of the province of the same name, covers a large space of ground. The houses were mostly of logs, but some were spacious and tolerably handsome, and surrounded with large gardens. The churches and other public buildings, with their cupolas, made quite a conspicuous and pleasing appearance as we approached the place, but the streets were irregular, unpaved, and muddy. The latitude of the town is 62° 30′ N.

The breadth of the Lena at Yakutsk is about two miles. This magnificent river takes its rise in the southern part of Siberia, in lat. 52°. Its general course is northeast, and it empties into the Arctic Ocean in lat. 75°. With its tributaries it forms the principal channel for the discharge of the great water-sheds of the eastern part of the empire, and the thoroughfare of communication with the provinces of Ochotsk, Kamtchatka and the Aleutian Islands. Down this stream vessels carried the various articles needed in those distant regions, such as bread-stuffs, liquors, and manufactures, and brought up in return the furs and other commodities which found a ready market in China and Russia.

VIII.

YAKUTSK. — DIFFERENT MODES OF TRAVELLING. — VOYAGE UP THE
LENA. — I ARRIVE AT IRKUTSK.

I DETERMINED to remain at Yakutsk a few days, to look around and ascertain the best mode of proceeding up the river to Irkutsk. The distance in a straight line was about 1500 miles, but by following the stream it would be much increased. There were post-stations the whole way, mostly on the left bank, and at intervals of twenty or thirty versts. At these horses were kept by the government, and one mode of making the proposed journey was in a small open boat, which was towed by them after the manner of a canal-boat, except that passengers changed boats at every station. Another mode, and that which I decided to adopt, was to hire a larger craft, with mast and sails, and perform the whole distance without changing; but I was to have the privilege of receiving assistance from the horses whenever necessary, and for this purpose I obtained an order from the government called a *deroshner* or *poderoshner*.

As soon as I had come to this conclusion, I commenced a search for a suitable boat, and at the same time I took the opportunity to look round the town. Accompanied by one of the gentlemen of the establishment, who devoted himself to my service, I visited all the public places, including the monastery, churches, and forts. I also called on several families, and was introduced as an American captain. Some of them were very inquisitive, and anxious to know where America was. It was a mystery to them how I got there, if I did not come by the way of St. Petersburg and Moscow. I explained as well as I could without an interpreter, but after all they appeared to be rather sceptical. The Commandant, a cheerful and clever old man, was very kind and obliging, and we exchanged several visits. He asked for information with regard to our government and constitution, which I explained as well as I could; and as he understood no English and I very little Russ, it is quite possible I was taken for a very knowing chap. When I made a call at any one's house, no matter what time of day it was, if I stayed long enough for the tea-kettle to boil (which, by the by, was almost always kept boiling), I was asked to take a cup of tea, and it was considered almost an insult to refuse. The second cup was usually laced with a little ardent spirits. This tea-drinking I found to be the universal custom in Siberia.

The sables collected in the vicinity of Yakutsk are the finest and most beautiful in the world, and command a much higher price than those from Kamtchatka. As I had already collected a few skins as specimens, in my travels, I requested the Superintendent of the Company's establishment to supply me with a pair of the very best this district produced, and he kindly complied. They were certainly of great beauty, very dark-colored and shiny, with very long and thick-set fur.

I found a boat in a few days, belonging to a couple of itinerant merchants, who had come down in her from the head-waters of the river, which I thought would answer my purpose. It was quite a nice boat, of about twenty feet in length; a little aft the centre there was a small round-house, with a sleeping-berth on each side. It had a keel, but was of light draft. The mast carried one large square sail; and we could row with two oars forward and two aft. I chartered the boat for the passage, and was to deliver it up to the merchants, or their agent, when we had arrived at head-waters. One man who came down in it was to return with me, on condition he worked his passage; and I found that the owners themselves desired to accompany us to their home. I had no serious objection to this, provided they supplied their own provisions; and, in fact, I thought it might be rather an advantage, as they were acquainted with the river. I gave them to understand at the outset, however, that the cabin must be at my exclusive disposal, and to this they readily agreed. I accordingly sent on board my goods and chattels, cooking utensils, and provisions. The Commandant, at my request, very obligingly appointed a Cossack to go with me, and a smart, energetic little fellow he was.

Having made everything ready, I took leave of my friends in Yakutsk, and assumed the command of my little craft, on the morning of the 30th of July, and thus commenced what was to me an entirely new phase of navigation. The wind being adverse, I had the horses hitched on, and away we went. My crew consisted of my man Parker, Kutsnetsoff, the Cossack, the man who worked his passage, and together with the two merchants and myself made seven of us in all. My weapons of defence (of which, by the way, there did not seem to be much need) consisted of a pair of double-barrelled pistols with spring bayonets, and a large broadsword, with a conspicuous gilt hilt finished off with an eagle's head. These implements looked dreadfully formidable and warlike, and I deposited them in a convenient place in my cabin. I assigned to Parker, Kutsnetsoff, and the Cossack the berth which I did not use, and they were to turn in and out by watches. The two merchants and the other man were to select the best place to sleep they could find elsewhere. With matters arranged in this way, we went on in good style, the horses going most of the time at a gentle trot. In the course of the day we passed two post-stations.

On the morning of the second day, having accomplished about 150 versts of my journey, I stopped at a post-station, where the official appeared to be a much more wide-awake man than any we had passed. I sent my *deroshner* to be written on, and my Cossack ordered the horses to be attached. This order not being obeyed at once, I saw there was some difficulty, and sent Kutsnetsoff to see what was the matter. On returning, he asked me to go into the office myself. So, hauling up the collar of my shirt, and, assuming such an air of importance as I thought the case might require, I went and demanded the cause of my detention. "The horses are all ready for you, Sir," said the postilion, "but those two merchants cannot go in that boat. The government don't keep horses to accommodate travelling traders. If they want horses, they must pay for them." There was no alternative, but that the fellows should leave the boat; and, to my surprise, they did it without a word of objection. Perhaps they were conscious that they had taken advantage of my ignorance to get a passage home free of charge. I was not sorry for their removal, although they appeared to be good men; for one of them was a constant singer of love-songs which were all High Dutch to me, and from his proximity to my quarters his well-intended music became very annoying. This difficulty removed, we proceeded again, under three horse-power. By the time we reached the next station, the wind became favorable, we hoisted our sail to the breeze, and cast off from the horses. By keeping near the shore, out of the main current, we made better progress in this way than we had done previously, and passed several stations without stopping. And so we went on by sail or by horse-power, according as the winds were favorable or adverse.

August 6th, we reached Olakminsk, which is about 600 versts from Yakutsk. By this time I began to think the mode of travelling I had chosen very pleasant. The season was delightful, and the scenery as we passed along was diversified with objects of sublimity and beauty. At times we were moving through level country, and at times among high mountains; in some places the river was contracted to a narrow span by precipitous ranges of cliffs, and again its broad expanse embraced many islands. To relieve the monotony of the confinement on board my boat, I occasionally rode on horseback from one station to another, and found the change very agreeable. The country in some places was thick-wooded, chiefly with fir and birch; in others, it was clothed with shrubbery, and I noticed currant and gooseberry bushes, and frequently alighted to refresh myself with the fruit. We passed a number of small clusters of shanties, inhabited by Tunguscans, in the vicinity of which herds of cattle were grazing. Near the houses were domestic reindeer of a large size. The children were playing about in little groups, and the older ones were amusing the younger by holding them on the backs of the deer, and teaching them to ride, — making quite a rural and domestic scene.

We had at no time on our route any lack of good milk, and once we had about a gallon of rich cream given us. The idea struck me that it might be converted into butter; I therefore had it put into a large pot, and with a kind of pudding-stick sat down at my cabin door, and as we were moving along began to stir it. In the course of half an hour I produced a lump of butter that would have put to shame seven eighths of the dairy-maids in this country.

I had long since noticed the great deference shown to the military in these parts, but I saw it particularly illustrated by my Cossack, in exerting his authority among the people at a post-station. He was scolding them for their laziness in hitching on the horses, and I could hear that he was making a very great lion of me. "Start quick, you rascals," said he, "we have got a great American captain in the boat, going on government business!" And this seemed to accelerate everything, even the horses, for they travelled better after it.

On the 15th, we passed Witim, which is about 1,400 versts from Yakutsk. Here the favorable winds, of which we had availed ourselves for several days past, left us, and we took, as usual, to horse-power. A short time after, we came to a station of some ten or twelve houses, where the inhabitants were in great perturbation on account of the small-pox, which was raging among them. Some had fled from the place, and others would have gone had they not been detained by their families. The disease existed among them in all its stages, from the symptoms to the full pox. I had had considerable experience with it, and thought I might mitigate the suffering by inoculation. They were all desirous that I should do so, and gathered anxiously around me. I called for a needle and thread, and selecting one of the subjects whose pox was ripe, drew the thread through the pustules until it was saturated with matter. Then preparing the maggot (as I believe it is called), by cutting the thread into very short pieces, with my penknife I made a little incision in the upper arm, placed in it one of the maggots and bound it there. I went through this process on seven or eight, and instructed them how to perform it; and as to their diet, to eat no fat or salt meat, but to confine themselves to bread and milk. They were very grateful for the advice, and for what I had done for them, and were desirous of manifesting their gratitude in some more substantial form, but it was declined.

After passing through an extensive grazing country, interspersed with large fields of grain, about 300 versts from Witim we came to rapids, with high precipitous banks on either side, where the velocity of the current was so great that we were obliged to hug the shore to avoid it. In some parts of it we could only get along by sending a small boat ahead to carry a line to warp by. This was a slow and laborious operation, and we were heartily rejoiced when we were through with it. The rapids once passed, the scenery soon became as interesting as it had been before, and the country, if anything, rather more populous and thriving. We saw, beside farming and grazing, a number of men engaged in fisheries along the banks of the stream. I could not see but that there was as great a degree of happiness here as in any other part of the world. The wants of the people were abundantly provided for by the produce of the soil and the river, and beyond this they seemed to have no desire.

After passing through some more rapids, where we were again obliged to cast off our horses and warp the boat, on the 19th we reached Kirinsk, which is about 1,650 versts from Yakutsk. From here we went on quickly, owing to the good path for the horses on the shore, and on the 26th reached Wercholinsk. This was a considerable town, situated on the right bank of the Lena; but we pushed by it without stopping. We now began to be troubled with the shallowness of the water, but we made out with difficulty to reach Katschuk, beyond which there was hardly enough to float a canoe, and we concluded we had reached the head of navigation. According to agreement I delivered up my boat here, and took a post-carriage for Irkutsk, where I arrived on the afternoon of the 28th of August, 1807, and drove into the court square of the Company's establishment.

IX.

IRKUTSK. — JOURNEY TO TOMSK. — NEW TRAVELLING COMPANION. — TOBOLSK. — RUSSIAN LEAVE-TAKING.

I PRESENTED my letters of introduction from the Chamberlain, Baron von Resanoff, and was kindly welcomed by the Superintendent. He invited me to make his house my home while I remained in the place. I replied that my stay must be short, and begged him to assist me in procuring a convenient vehicle for my journey, so that I might not be obliged to change at every station, as I should if I went in a public conveyance.

I discharged my Cossack when I gave up my boat, and made him a present of fifty rubles, all my cooking utensils, provisions, and some other articles. He took his leave, with many thanks and good wishes, which I cordially returned. I had brought Kutsnetsoff home to his native town, from which he had been absent ten years. He started off immediately to find his mother. The next morning he made his appearance at my room, leading her in. She was a very dignified-looking elderly lady, dressed in black. As he introduced her to me, she dropped upon her knees, and, while the tears from an overflowing and grateful heart were coursing down her cheeks, poured out her thanks for the interest I had taken in the return of her son. It touched me so deeply, that I could scarcely refrain from tears myself. It carried my thoughts home to my poor mother, and I raised her up, and assured her that, if I had done her son a favor, or brought comfort and consolation to her, I was amply compensated by the pleasure and satisfaction the deed itself afforded me. Kutsnetsoff had previously observed that he should like to go on with me to Moscow to see his brother, if his mother were willing. When it was suggested to her, she readily gave her consent, being also desirous that he should see his brother.

While we were talking about the matter, who should drive into the court square but Dr. Langsdorff. I was rejoiced to see him, but could not account for his being so close upon my heels. It appeared that he had arrived at Yakutsk shortly after my departure, and, making but a short stay, had been pushing on in the small boats, hoping to overtake and surprise me on the river. He had gained two days on me, but encountered all kinds of troubles and vexations, such as leaky boats, drunken boatmen, an inefficient Cossack guide, the upsetting of the boat, and loss of papers. He was quite chagrined when I told him that I, by taking a larger craft under my own control, had avoided all these difficulties, and had made quite a pleasant excursion of it.

The Doctor having decided to make a longer stay than I desired to, that he might visit Kiakta, across the Lake Baikal, I purchased a vehicle which I thought would answer my purpose. It was called a *pervoshka*, and was nothing more than a box rounded at the bottom, and fixed firmly to the axletree without springs. A covered top reached from the back part nearly to the middle, resembling the top of a cradle. The forward part of the box was covered far enough to make a seat for the driver, from which a boot extended to the cradle-top. On the bottom of this outlandish concern I must either lie or sit upright throughout my whole journey. I therefore procured a good substantial feather-bed and put it in, with which and two or three well-stuffed pillows, my luggage, and other wadding, I thought I might get along without much chafing. As this carriage was only calculated for one person, I took a post-carriage of much the same construction for Parker and Kutsnetsoff.

Being now all ready for the road, I decided to stay a day or two, and look round the place with my friend the Doctor. I shall not attempt a description of this large, and I might say handsome town. It is the modern capital of Siberia, and is situated on the banks of the beautiful river Angara, which is one of the largest tributaries of the Yenisei. It was in that day, and I suppose still is, the great commercial emporium of the eastern part of the empire, whence the more distant provinces are supplied, and whither are brought the furs and the products of the fisheries from Kamtchatka, Ochotsk, and the Aleutian Islands; and through the frontier town of Kiakta, across Lake Baikal, the teas, nankins, silks, and other articles which are obtained from the Chinese in exchange for the sea-otter and sable skins, and find such a ready market in Russia.

Having a journey before me of 3,500 miles, and desirous of reaching St. Petersburg before the close of navigation in the autumn, I was prepared to travel day and night, and of course passed many towns and villages without noticing them, only making short halts for a day or two at some of the larger or shire-towns to rest. I was provided with a new *deroshner*, and a good supply of copper money to pay for fresh post-horses. On the 31st of August, having hitched the horses to our vehicles, — that is, one in the shafts of each, and one on each side, — and having again taken leave of Doctor Langsdorff and the Company's Superintendent, the Yemshik, as the driver is called, mounted his box, cracked his whip, and away we went, leaving the capital of Siberia behind us. The post-stations were about 25 versts, or 15 miles, asunder, and we were well attended at them. If we desired it, we could obtain something to eat, and I generally availed myself of the opportunity twice a day, taking a substantial meal, and topping off with a cup of tea, preparatory for which we almost always found the kettle boiling. The Yemshik's signal for starting was the crack of his whip, and at that the horses would bound off at full speed, and he would begin to sing. The song, as well as the speed, was generally kept up from one station to another. The music was sometimes quite pleasant and cheering; the horses, at any rate, seemed to know that it meant "Go ahead."

In this way we continued night and day. On the 6th of September we passed through Krasnojarsk, where the Chamberlain Baron von Resanoff had died. We continued on without stopping, and on the 7th reached the town of Poim, where I halted a couple of hours to deliver a letter from the young man Chlabnekoff, whom I took as a passenger from Kamtchatka to Ochotsk, to his brother. He called on me, and insisted on my going to his house, if it was only for an hour. His family wanted to see me. I took Kutsnetsoff with me, and we gave them all the information we could about their brother. We found a splendid collation prepared for us, with Madeira wine such as we do not have in these days. After concluding the entertainment with a bottle of champagne, we started off; and whatever the facts may have been, we certainly felt much lighter than before. I merely mention this circumstance to show that there was no lack of "the good stuff" in Siberia. The Maine Law was not enforced there half a century ago.

On the 10th I reached the shire-town of Tomsk, and was constrained to acknowledge myself pretty well used up. I can assure those who have not made a trial of this mode of travelling, that to lay on one's back in a carriage without any springs, for eight days and nights in succession, is no joke. When I alighted occasionally my whole frame was in a perfect tremor, yet the roads were not stony, but tolerably good. There was no regular hotel in the town, and so after a little inquiry we drove up to a large log-house, with a square enclosure in front, the owner of which was kind enough to entertain us. I immediately set Kutsnetsoff upon the lookout for a more easy and convenient carriage, and told him if he should find one to endeavor to dispose of my old one in part pay. In the mean time, having a letter from my friend Lieutenant Schwostoff to his uncle, who was Governor of the place, I waited on him. I was very cordially received, and invited to dine the next day.

In a short time Kutsnetsoff succeeded in finding a vehicle much better than the old one. It was quite a stylish affair, on springs, and two persons could ride in it conveniently; but I had to pay as much to boot, perhaps, as both carriages were worth. I called upon the Company's agent to furnish me with 200 rubles, but he had received no particular instructions to advance me money, and was reluctant to do it. He was quite reasonable, however, and was willing to listen to my story. While I was explaining to him who I was, and why I wanted money, there were several persons standing by. Among them was a good-looking, well-dressed man, who spoke up and said he would let me have as large a sum as I wanted, at which the agent said he was willing to supply me. After I had finished my business the gentleman who made the kind offer of his purse informed me that he himself was going to Moscow, and, if I had no objections, would like to take a seat in my carriage, and share the expense. I hardly knew what to answer, and I scrutinized him very closely. His face wore an honest look, and he had about his person two conspicuous orders of merit; so I concluded to accept his proposition. I found no reason afterwards to regret it. He was a Greek by birth, and a merchant of high standing. His name was Dementy Simonitch, and he had done several meritorious acts, for which he received medals from the Emperor Alexander, and likewise a present from him of a splendid gold watch and chain.

Having arranged this matter, I repaired to the Governor's to dine and take leave of him. I found a great many gentlemen there, but not one who spoke English, so that I was almost a dummy amongst them. I understood enough Russ, however, to learn that they were desirous of inquiring into the nature and organization of our government. I explained all the prominent points as well as I could, and they appeared to understand, for they praised our institutions highly. If I was able, under the circumstances, to form a correct opinion, there was a good deal of the spirit of reform among them. After taking leave of the Governor, I commenced preparations to start the next morning. As I saw but little of the town, I can say but little or nothing of it. It was quite a large place, the houses nearly all of wood, and the streets broad and in some places planked in the centre for the convenience of foot-travel, and yet in others so muddy that there was no comfort in moving round out of a carriage.

On the 12th of September I started with my new companion, and went on at the same breakneck pace as before. My new coach was far superior to the old one. We could sit up or lie down as we chose, and were not annoyed by the intolerable jarring of the body. My companion was very agreeable, and although he could not speak a word of English, and my vocabulary of Russ was too limited to hold a continued, intelligible conversation, we soon became accustomed to each other's pantomimic gestures, and got along quite understandingly. On the 19th we arrived, without any casualties worthy of remark, at Tobolsk, the ancient capital of Siberia, and put up, as usual, at a private house.

Here my carriage-mate, Dementy, had acquaintances. He introduced me to the family of Mr. Zelinzoff, or Green, a highly respectable and wealthy merchant, and the proprietor of large iron-works at Ekatereinburg. He was himself absent from home, but, together with Dementy, I was invited by his son, who officiated as major-domo, to dine with his family while I remained in the city. I take pleasure in particularizing in regard to this family, on account of their marked civility and kindness to a stranger. It consisted of Madam Zelinzoff, three sons, a daughter, and a young man named Duro, who was a teacher of French, and spoke English fluently. They lived in splendid style, and spread a table for fifteen or twenty persons every day. Among the numerous invited guests was a French military officer in the Russian service, who spoke English well, and with whom I had a good deal of chat. After dinner the ladies and gentlemen retired to a large hall, where there was a billiard-table and a piano, violins and flutes, on which the amateurs displayed their skill. This was the agreeable practice daily while I was there.

Perhaps I may be allowed here to make a few remarks in regard to the city of Tobolsk, though I cannot give a minute description of it. It is very singularly divided into the upper and lower town. The lower town seems to have been once the bed of the river Irtich, which now, uniting with the Tobol, runs through the western part of the valley, leaving both the upper and lower town on the eastern side, but divided distinctly by a steep bank, which was probably in former days the margin of the stream. The lower town is sometimes, though rarely, inundated; and on the other hand the upper town is inconvenienced by a want of water. Taking both sections together they formed a very large place, with a numerous and mixed population of Tartars, Bucharians, and Kalmucks. The public buildings were mostly of stone, but the private houses, with few exceptions, of wood. It was the great mart of trade with the eastern part of the Empire, and all the caravans from China and the distant provinces concentrated here.

This place had formerly been the Botany Bay, or penal settlement, of the Russians, and from the descendants of convicts a great and flourishing city had sprung up, with its wealthy merchants, thrifty traders, and literary and scientific men. The German and French languages were taught and spoken by all the better classes. All kinds of provisions were so cheap, that the poorest inhabitant never need suffer for food; and I could see here, as throughout Siberia, the kindliest feelings manifested toward the lower orders of society.

Having remained at Tobolsk six days, we prepared to continue our journey. Two of the young Mr. Zelinzoffs were to accompany us as far as their father's estate, at Ekatereinburg. Accordingly, after dining and making some preliminary arrangements for departure, the whole family, with their guests, assembled in the large room for a little chat and to take leave. Now this leave-taking was a somewhat formal piece of business, and I had misgivings as to how I should acquit myself with becoming gallantry. The custom with the gentlemen was for each to lay the right hand on the other's back, and to kiss each other on both cheeks; not unfrequently the noses came in rude collision. A lady presents you the back of the hand to kiss, and at the same time she kisses you on the cheek. Being all ready for action, the ladies and gentlemen placed themselves in a row round the room, and then the performance was commenced by the two sons who were going with us, and continued by my friend Dementy. By this time the perspiration had begun to start upon my forehead; but I saw it was of no use to be lagging, and so, summoning all my courage, I turned to, and went through the ceremony like a veteran courtier. The last of the ladies I came to was the daughter, a great beauty, and I was greatly tempted, in violation of Russian etiquette, to kiss her cheek, but I managed to restrain myself.

X.

FLYING FERRY-BOAT. — EKATEREINBURG. — KAZAN. — A DINNER-PARTY. — MOSCOW. — ST. PETERSBURG. — GOOD NEWS.

AFTER the ceremony described in the last chapter, we took to our carriages and proceeded to the ferry which crosses the Irtich, where we found what was called a flying ferry-boat, of sufficient size to transport several teams at once. The hull of the craft did not swim deep in the water, but was furnished with a very deep keel along its whole length. It had a short mast, placed about as far forward as in sloops, and supported by shrouds. Now an anchor was sunk in the centre of the river some distance above, and from the anchor a rope, sustained on the surface by buoys, was extended and fastened to the bow of the boat. By means of a block and pulley this rope could be elevated about half the distance to the mast-head. When ready for starting, the bow, which was always pointed directly up stream at the landing-place, was pushed off a little, so that the current might strike the keel at an angle.

This position was maintained by the use of the rudder; and as the boat could not drift down the river, on account of the anchor to which it was attached, it was driven sideways to the opposite shore. By this ingenious contrivance passengers and freight were carried across without the least trouble or labor.

On the 24th we arrived at Ekatereinburg. During our stay here of one night, our young friends showed us about the iron-works, and we saw all the operations, from smelting the ore to working it up into bar-iron. Gold ore was dug here by the government, and the pure metal extracted by pulverizing, and washing it on an inclined plane covered with ridges, which stopped the gold, while the lighter substances were carried off with the water. It did not appear to be a very money-making process. The next day we took leave of our young friends, and pursued our journey westward to Kazan, on the river Volga, which we reached on the 30th. Here my carriage-mate, Dementy, was quite at home again, and we concluded to halt for a couple of days. The city was large and well built, and the most important place in the eastern part of Russia proper.

I had for some time experienced the good

effects of Dementy's badge of distinction, but it did us especial service here. It procured us an invitation to dine with the military Governor, who was himself of Greek extraction, and somewhat acquainted with my friend. I had no great desire to go among great folks, as my wardrobe was scanty, and the few clothes I possessed had grown pretty threadbare with the wear and tear of my three years' cruise. I wished to decline, but Dementy said it would give offence. He had probably given an account of my adventures, and of my negotiation with the Chamberlain, Baron von Resanoff; and this, together with the mark of the Emperor's approbation which he himself wore, had brought us into notice.

At the proper time the military carriage of the Governor came for us, and away we went in fine style. We found a great number of persons assembled at his house, including officers, military and civil, and many ladies. I was introduced as an American captain. I felt a little uncomfortable lest I should be questioned with regard to my official grade, as it might not have been good policy to have explained my claim to a captaincy. It was a splendid entertainment, however, and, as I could not converse very intelligibly, I had little else to do than ply the knife and fork, while

Dementy, who had somehow picked up all the particulars about me and my business, gave them my whole story, much to my satisfaction. After dinner we retired to another room, where coffee was served. The ladies questioned me about our country, and to show that they had some knowledge of American history, they spoke of Washington and Franklin in high terms. We conversed upon the subject until I had exhausted my whole stock of Russ in eulogizing those men.

October 2d, we started on our route for Moscow, our next stopping-place. We met with nothing remarkable excepting muddy roads and frequent altercations at the post-stations. There was evidently less respect paid to my friend's decorations, and less alacrity in attending to us. We, however, reached the great city of Moscow on the 8th, and passed within the first circle, which is called the Zemlänoigorod. We wound along through the streets, as it seemed to me, for miles. At last Dementy pointed out a public house, where we stopped awhile to brush up and make ourselves look respectable,—after which Dementy left us. Kutsnetsoff sought at once the whereabouts of the Company's establishment, and we started again, passed through the

Bale gate into the circle of that name, and drove to the Company's house. I entered the spacious stone building with Kutsnetsoff, and met his brother, the Superintendent, on the great landing-stair. He was a splendid-looking man. After the brothers had embraced each other, and while tears were rolling down their cheeks, I was introduced. I was cordially welcomed, and led into a large hall, where I was presented to the Superintendent's lady, and Kutsnetsoff to a sister he had never seen before. She was a very handsome woman, and richly dressed in the latest French style.

After exchanging mutual inquiries, I was told by the Superintendent that his house must be my home while I remained in the city. I replied that I was desirous of reaching St. Petersburg before the close of navigation, and consequently my stay must be short. They concluded that I could well spare a week. In that time I thought I could replenish my wardrobe with the latest European fashions, and at my request, a draper was sent for; he took my dimensions, and I was soon fitted out completely. My Kamtchatka sable-skins were converted into a lining for a great coat,—as something of that kind had now become necessary,—and they made a splendid article.

In the mean time, having leisure, I availed myself of the politeness of a young gentleman of the house, who offered to go round with me and show me the city. I made no note of what I saw at the time, and since then half a century has rolled by. I can only recall some of the leading features of the great metropolis, which may be interesting, as the date of my visit was but a few years before the conflagration which drove Napoleon from the country. The city is situated on an elevation which in shape resembles a turtle's back. The river Moskva sweeps round nearly two thirds of it, and the land rises gently from the margin to the centre, which is so high as to command a splendid panoramic view of its whole extent. The city was divided into four departments or circles. The first, the Kremlin, situated on the crown of this eminence, and enclosed with heavy ramparts of stone, formed a sort of fortress of very ample extent. It embraced within its walls magnificent cathedrals, palaces, and public buildings, all gorgeously decorated. Here also was the great bell, which stands on the ground, with a triangular piece broken out of the rim. Its weight is said to be four hundred thousand pounds. The next circle was the Kitaigorod, or Chinese Town, also containing several cathedrals, convents, parish churches, and many noblemen's houses, interspersed with mean-looking wooden buildings. The third circle, which surrounded the former, was the Beloigorod, or White Town, and had a white wall. This was the business part of the city, and the streets, though mostly paved, were muddy and filthy. There were here, however, many public edifices, and handsome private houses, the residences of the merchants and traders. The fourth circle, called Zemlänoigorod, or Land Town, was surrounded with an earthen embankment, and enclosed an area of nearly ten miles. In this as in the other circles, there was a great diversity in the cost of the different structures, the very extremes of magnificence and meanness being mingled together promiscuously. I was very much impressed with the grandeur and beauty of the whole city; spread over more than twenty square miles of ground, adorned with a countless number of costly and elegant buildings, with thousands of spires and cupolas covered with silver and gold, when viewed from the Kremlin it afforded one of the most pleasing spectacles I ever gazed upon.

I was loath to leave when the time allotted

for my stay had expired, but there was no help for it. So, equipped in the fashionable rig with which the draper furnished me, I turned my face toward St. Petersburg. The Superintendent was kind enough to propose that Kutsnetsoff should accompany me to my journey's end, which proposal I gladly accepted. On the morning of the 17th, I took leave of the good friends who had shown me so much kindness, and stepped into my carriage, rode through the suburbs, and at noon emerged into the open country. We passed many villages and large towns, but continued on without stopping at any of them except to take our meals.

On the 21st of October, 1807, we reached the gates of St. Petersburg, and, after going through a thorough examination of passports, were permitted to go on. We drove at once to the Company's establishment, where I was kindly received and entertained by Mr. Booldakoff, the first director of the Russian American Company. It was evening when I arrived, and as neither Mr. B. nor any one in the house could speak English, I remained partially ignorant of the business which most interested me until the next morning. A gentleman then came in who accosted me in good round English, and I was quite overjoyed at the sound. This was Mr. Benedict Cramer, a gentleman with whom I became very intimate in business afterwards. He was the senior partner of the house of Cramer, Smith, & Co., and was also one of the directors of the Company.

He soon threw light upon my whole business by saying that his partner, Mr. Smith, was in the United States, and had seen my owners and assured them that the bills of exchange, the duplicates of which had reached them through the hands of Mr. Moorfield, were good. Mr. Moorfield had been out with a ship in the course of the season, the bills had been accepted and paid with fifteen per cent advance, because Spanish dollars, in which they were payable, commanded that premium. The proceeds had been invested in hemp, iron, and manufactures and sent to America; and the business had been transacted through his house. "You have now nothing to do," he concluded, "but to take all the pleasure you can while you remain with us." I shook him heartily by the hand, and made him a low bow; after which we walked out together to his place of business. He introduced me to his brother and

Mr. L. Harris, the American Consul, who was connected with his firm; and in the same way I became acquainted with a number of influential gentlemen, from whom I received many civilities.

Mr. Booldakoff, whose house I made my home, showed me every attention. He took me in his carriage to all the places of note in the city, and had an audience with the Count Ramansoff, the Prime Minister, to whom I was presented. In short, every mark of respect that could be accorded to a stranger was shown me.

XI.

I SAIL DOWN THE BALTIC IN A DUTCH GALIOT. — TAKE PASSAGE AT ELSINORE IN THE MARY FOR PORTLAND. — PUT IN AT LIVERPOOL. — HOME AGAIN. — CONCLUSION.

THINGS went on so smoothly and pleasantly at St. Petersburg that I took no note of time. Six days had already slipped by before I began to think of making a further move. There were no American ships at Cronstadt when I arrived, but I was told that there were always opportunities till the last of November to obtain a passage to England, so that I felt quite easy. Just as I commenced preparations for starting, however, war was declared between Russia and England, and all foreign ships left Cronstadt. I now thought it doubtful whether I could obtain a passage to England, but I made all haste for the port, to make a trial, at least. Mr. Booldakoff gave me a letter to the harbor-master, the Consul one to his Vice, the Messrs. Cramer one to Messrs. Belfour, Ellah, & Co., at Elsinore. With these I took leave of my St.

Petersburg friends, and started; but when I arrived at the Mole I was quite discouraged to find that there was not a merchant-vessel in sight. I called on the Vice-Consul, but he knew of no way to help me. Though thinking it would be useless, I determined to present my letter to the harbor-master. He read it, and after a little reflection, and a number of questions about my journey, said that I had better go down to the Mole head with him, and see what could be done.

We found, on inquiry, that there was one solitary vessel, a small galiot, lying at anchor below the Tolbeacon, about three miles off. She was bound for London, and he thought I could get a passage in her, if I were willing to try; at the same time he offered to send me aboard. I jumped at the proposition, and told Parker to get our goods and chattels into the boat as soon as possible. Thanking the harbor-master for his assistance, I started off for the galiot. She was a small craft, of seventy or eighty tons burden, loaded with tallow. The skipper was a little old Dutchman, short of five feet in height, and a mate and cook composed his crew. I asked him if he would take me as passenger to London. " Yaw," says he. " And will you let my man work his passage ?" " Yaw, goot," says he. I paid the officer of the boat for his trouble, and he left us. Being now at leisure, I began to look round to see what kind of a ship and accommodations we had got. She was rather a flat-bottomed vessel, carrying lee-boards, to keep her from drifting to the leeward when sailing by the wind. I questioned the skipper about the provisions, and he believed that there were enough, such as they were. The cabin was a trunk, so called, above the deck, abaft the mainmast, in which there were two boxes with slide-doors. One was his berth, and the other the mate's. He informed me that I must sleep with him, and my man must turn in and out with the mate. I thought this a fair arrangement, and so we settled it.

It was morning when I went on board; and after dinner, which consisted of beans and buckwheat pudding, we got under way. The wind was light but favorable, so that we crept along down the Gulf at about the same rate we used to go in our little Russian vessel. The weather was moderate and the sea smooth, and after so much land-travel I enjoyed the change very much. We continued to grope along until we reached the island of Bornholm, in the Baltic. Here we took a westerly gale, which would have put a stop to our progress if we had not fortunately got under the lee of the island, and continued sailing from one end to the other of it for two days, when the gale abated, and the wind changed. This enabled us to continue on our course, so that on the 13th of November we reached Elsinore. Here I presented my letters from the Messrs. Cramer, and was kindly received by Messrs. Belfour, Ellah, & Co.

Though the galiot was detained by contrary winds, as long as there was no alternative, I concluded to stick by her; but on the second day I was standing on the pier and looking up the sound towards Copenhagen, when I saw a ship coming down with a large American ensign flying, at the sight of which my heart leaped right up into my throat. I waited until she came to anchor, and then called a shore-boat and went off to her. She proved to be the Mary of Portland, Captain David Gray, and was homeward bound. This was joyful news, and affected me so deeply that I could hardly tell the Captain my story. At last, after making known who I was, and from whence I came, I asked him if he would take me as passenger, and he readily consented. I went immediately to the galiot to settle with the little Dutch skipper. To the question, how much was I to pay him, he answered that he only wanted "Was billig ist, das ist mir recht." Not knowing exactly what that was, I tendered him twenty Spanish dollars, with which he was well satisfied, and made him a bonus of a pair of leather breeches, which he had worn ever since we left Cronstadt. Wishing him a prosperous voyage, I took my leave and my baggage and went on board the Mary. She was a fine ship, in ballast, and had a splendid cabin for the times. The captain was a social, clever fellow, and we soon became well acquainted. We left Elsinore on the 20th, and proceeded down the Kattegat. When we got down as far as Gottenburg, we found the wind blowing in heavily through Sleeve, which obliged the pilot to put into Marstrand, a small port in Sweden. Here we lay two days.

On the 24th, we put to sea again. We passed the Naze of Norway, and steered for the Orkney Islands; but, owing to adverse winds and stormy weather, it was the 2d of December before we got through Fair Isle Passage. We then encountered a series of westerly gales, in the course of which it was discovered that one of the ship's rudder-braces had worked loose. It was deemed unsafe to pursue our course across the Atlantic, and Captain Gray accordingly altered his course for Liverpool, where we arrived on the 15th. This was a great disappointment to me, particularly as my pecuniary resources were exhausted, and I saw before me unavoidable expenses; at the same time, I had no relish for the storms of a northern passage and a winter's coast. I reconciled myself, however, with the prospect of seeing England; and as Captain Gray offered to supply me with money until I reached Portland, I was quite content. I went with him to a boarding-house, where we remained while the ship was undergoing repairs. In the mean time, I made myself acquainted with the city and its environs. At the end of two months the Mary was ready for sea again, and, having taken on board a quantity of salt, we sailed on the 7th of February. We had a pleasant voyage, and arrived at Portland on the 25th of March. Here I settled with the Captain, to whom I was indebted for my passage, board, and sundry loans, the whole amounting to the sum of two hundred and fifty dollars. I gave him a draft on Mr. John Park, of Boston, and it proved quite fortunate for him that I did so. His owners had failed just before our arrival, and, as they were indebted to him, he would have been a loser but for this draft.

You may suppose that I started with as little delay as possible for Bristol. I arrived there on the 1st of April, 1808, and thus terminated an absence of three years and eight months. In two years and six months from the time of my departure, the owners were in receipt of the proceeds of the voyage, which resulted in a clear profit of ONE HUNDRED THOUSAND DOLLARS.

I have now reached the end of my story; but before I lay down my pen, let me say a word more of the friends mentioned in the preceding pages. I continued in the Russian trade, in which I had made so successful a beginning, and returned to St. Petersburg in 1809. It so happened that I found Dr. Langsdorff and Lieutenants Schwostoff and Davidoff there. The latter two gentlemen, since we last met, had been engaged in the war with Sweden, and had become honorably distinguished. While I was visiting the Doctor, they came over to pass an evening with us, and we sat talking of old times until two in the morning. They then started for their own lodgings, which were on the other side of the river. Langsdorff and myself accompanied them to the drawbridge, which was open for ships to pass in the night. Our friends, therefore, passed over a plank which lay from the bridge to a vessel in the river and regained the other side of the bridge by another plank, calling to us and wishing us good-night, when they were safe over, and we then went back to our quarters. The next morning we received the melancholy intelligence that two naval officers had been drowned in the Neva during the night, and, upon further inquiry, we learned that they were our friends. After we had parted from them, they became desirous, God knows for what purpose, to return to us again, and, in order to get over quicker, they attempted to spring from the bridge upon a bark that was going through. They mistook a sail for the deck of the vessel, and both fell into the water. The people in the bark endeavored to rescue them, but the night was so dark, and the current so strong, that they went under before they received any assistance. Though fifty years have gone by since the death of these young men, I cannot forbear to recall their many virtues and lament their untimely end.

www.ingramcontent.com/pod-product-compliance
Lightning Source LLC
Chambersburg PA
CBHW030343170426
43202CB00010B/1217